Korean Cooking

100+ Authentic Korean Dishes to Cook at Home

Jiu Chung

Table of Contents

Introduction 10
Introduction to Korean Cuisine 12
   Location: Where Korean Cooking Comes From 12
   Yin and Yang: A Philosophy of Balance 16
   Five Elements: Harmony of Flavors 18
The Korean Pantry 19
   Gochugaru (Korean Chili Powder) 19
   Gochujang (Korean Chili Paste) 20
   Method 20
   Doenjang (Fermented Soybean Paste) 21
   Ganjang (Soy Sauce) 21
   Chamgireum (Toasted Sesame Oil) 21
   Aekjeot (Fish Sauce) 22
   Cheongju (Rice Wine) 22
   Ssalsikcho (Rice Wine Vinegar) 23
   Kkae (Toasted Sesame Seeds) 23
   Chapsal (Glutinous or Sweet Rice Flour) 24
Korean Kitchen Tools 25
   Dolsot (Stone Bowl) 25
   Onggi (Clay Pot) 26
   Siru (Earthenware Steamer) 27
   Sujeo (Utensils) 27
   Tabletop Grill 28
   Rice Cooker 29
Korean Staples: Recipes & Guidelines for Common Dishes 30
   Bap (Rice) 30

Gukbap (Rice Soup) 32
Juk (Rice Porridge) 34
Bokkeum-bap (Fried Rice 1) 35
Mushroom Rice 37
Bibimbap (Rice Dish with Meat and Vegetables) 39
Tteok-bokki (Spicy Rice Cakes) 42
BibimGuksu (Spicy Noodle Dish) 44
Japchae (Glass Noodle Stir Fry) 46
MulNaengmyeon (Cold Noodle Soup) 48
Mandu (Dumplings 1) 51
Kimchi Mandu (Dumplings 2) 54
Bulgogi (Grilled Beef) 56
Bulgogi Sauce 58
Daweaji Bulgogi (Grilled Pork) 59
Dak Bulgogi (Grilled Chicken 1) 61
Dak Bulgogi (Grilled Chicken 2) 63
Galbi (Grilled Short Ribs) 65
Mulgogi Gochujang (Spicy Fish) 67
Kkanpung Saeu (Spicy and Sweet Shrimp) 68

Banchan: Shared Small Dishes for Every Meal 71
Bokkeum: Stir-Fried Dishes 72
   Hobak Bokkeum (Stir-fried Zucchini) 72
   Oi Bokkeum (Stir-fried cucumbers) 74
   Gaji Bokkeum (Stir-fried Eggplant) 75
   Myulchi Bokkeum (Stir-fried Anchovies) 77
Buchimgaeor Jeon (Korean Pancakes) 79
   Kimchi Buchimgae (Kimchi Pancake) 79

Pajeon (Scallion Pancake) 81
Hobak Buchimgae (Zucchini Pancakes) 83
Gamja Jeon (Potato Pancakes) 85
Pancake Dipping Sauce 87
Namul (Vegetables).. 88
Kongnamul Muchim (Seasoned Bean Sprouts) 89
Sigeumchi Namul (Blanched Spinach) 91
Gaji Namul (Steamed Eggplant)...................................92
Watercress Namul 93
Mu Namul (Stir-fried Radish) 94
Other Banchan 95
Kongjang (Dried Beans in Soy)................................... 96
Gamja Jorim (Braised Potatoes)...................................97
Dubu Jorim (Braised Tofu).. 99
Oi Muchim (Cucumber Salad) 101
Mu Saengchae (Spicy Radish Salad) 102
Putbaechu Doenjang Muchim (Soybean Paste Cabbage) 103
Goguma Mattang (Candied Sweet Potatoes)..............104
Soy Sauce Eggs 106
GimGui (Toasted Seaweed) 107
Ssamjang (Dipping Sauce)...109
Kimchi and Other Pickles 110
Kimchi 110
Traditional Cabbage Kimchi 111
Quick Kimchi... 113
Kkaekdugi (Radish Kimchi)..115

    Baek-kimchi (Chili free Kimchi or "White Kimchi") .. 116
    Dongkimchi (Winter Kimchi) 118
    Nabak-kimchi (Spring Kimchi)............................... 120
    Oisobagi (Cucumber Kimchi) 121
    Pakimchi (Scallion Kimchi) 122
    Kkaennip Kimchi (Perilla Leaf Kimchi) 123
  Jangajii 124
    Soy Sauce Pickles... 124
    Doenjang (Soybean) Pickles 126
    Brined Pickles.. 127
  Jjeotgal 128
Soups & Stews... 129
  Kimchi KongnamulGuk (Kimchi & Bean Sprout Soup) . 130
  Baechu Doengjang Guk (Cabbage Soup with Soybean Paste) 132
  Ganjaguk (Potato Soup) 134
  Tteokguk (Rice Cake Soup) 136
  Oi Naengguk (Cold Cucumber Soup) 138
  Dak Gomtang (Chicken Soup).................................... 140
  Yukgaejang (Spicy Beef and Vegetable Soup)............ 142
  Galbitang (Beef Short Rib Soup) 144
  Haemul Jeongol (Seafood Hot Pot)............................ 146
  Bulgogi Jeongol (Beef Hot Pot) 148
  Kimchi Jjigae (Kimchi Stew) 150
  Haemul Sundubu Jjigae (Seafood and Tofu Stew) 152
  Hobak Gochujang Jjigae (Spicy Zucchini Stew) 154
  Budae Jjigae (Army Stew) 156

- Saewoojuk (Shrimp and Rice Porridge) 158
- Desserts: Hangwa and Tteok 160
  - Hangwa 160
    - Dasik (Tea Cookies) 160
    - Green Tea Cookies 160
    - Gwapyeon (Fruit Jelly) 162
    - Jeonggwa (Fruit Jerky) 164
    - Yaksik (Sweet Rice with Nuts and Fruit) 166
    - Yugwa (Sweet Rice Crackers) 168
    - Yumil-gwa (Fried Dough Sweet) 170
    - Kkultarae (King's Candy) 172
    - Yeot-gangjeong (Sesame Candy) 174
  - Tteok 175
  - Steamed Tteok 175
    - Kongtteok (Bean tteok) 175
    - Jeungpyeon (Rice wine tteok) 177
    - Baekseolgi (Raisin tteok) 179
  - Pounded Tteok 180
    - Injeolmi (Sweet Beantteok) 180
    - Kkaeinjeolmi (Black Sesame tteok) 182
    - Danpatjuk (Sweet Bean & Rice Dumpling Soup) 182
  - Shaped Tteok 184
    - Songpyeon (Half-moon stuffed tteok) 184
    - Baram Tteok (Round stuffed tteok) 186
  - Pan Fried Tteok 187
    - Hwajeon (Flower tteok) 187
    - Bukkumi (Filled Crescent tteok) 189

Drinks 190
   Cha (Tea) 190
      Green Tea: How to Brew 191
      Barley Tea: How to Brew 191
      Fruit Teas: How to Brew 192
      Cinnamon Tea 193
   Non-Alcoholic Drinks 193
      Sujeonggwa (Cinnamon Ginger Punch) 193
      Subak Hwachae (Watermelon Punch) 193
      Sikhye (Sweet Rice Drink) 194
   Alcoholic Drinks 195
      Soju Yogurt Cocktail 196
      Flavored Liquors 196
      Ginger Cocktail 197
Conclusion 198

© **Copyright by Jiu Chung - All rights reserved.**

This Book is provided with the sole purpose of providing relevant information on a specific topic for which every reasonable effort has been made to ensure that it is both accurate and reasonable. Nevertheless, by purchasing this Book you consent to the fact that the author, as well as the publisher, are in no way experts on the topics contained herein, regardless of any claims as such that may be made within. As such, any suggestions or recommendations that are made within are done so purely for entertainment value. It is recommended that you always consult a professional prior to undertaking any of the advice or techniques discussed within.

This is a legally binding declaration that is considered both valid and fair by both the Committee of Publishers Association and the American Bar Association and should be considered as legally binding within the United States.

The reproduction, transmission, and duplication of any of the content found herein, including any specific or extended information will be done as an illegal act regardless of the end form the information ultimately takes. This includes copied versions of the work both physical, digital and audio unless express consent of the Publisher is provided beforehand. Any additional rights reserved.

Furthermore, the information that can be found within the pages described forthwith shall be considered both accurate and truthful when it comes to the recounting of facts. Therefore, any utilization, in any form - correct or otherwise, will make the Publisher free of responsibility as to the actions taken outside of their direct purview. Regardless, there are zero scenarios where the original author or the Publisher can be deemed liable in any fashion for any damages or hardships that may result from any of the information discussed in this document.

Furthermore, the contents of this document are solely for informative purposes only and hence should be regarded as universal. As such, the information is given without the guarantee of its validity or interim quality.

Trademarks that are mentioned are done without written consent and can in no way be considered an endorsement from the trademark holder. This document likewise provided trademarks without written consent, and should not be seen as advertisement from the trademark owner.

Introduction

The past decade has been a boon for lovers of international food, and Korean food, in particular, has benefitted from the explosion of interest in various Asian cuisines. Many so-called "foodies" are aware of the ubiquitous Korean "taco," food truck-style, and kimchi, perhaps Korea's most famous food export, regularly appears on restaurant menus and grocery store shelves alike.

What many people may not know is that traditional Korean cooking is both easy and satisfying to prepare at home. With its warming spices and chili pastes, its generous use of garlic and fermented foods, and its welcoming traditions of many shared dishes, Korean cuisine is a justifiably renowned family friendly style of eating. While Korean food shares some elements with Japanese and Chinese cooking, its bold flavors, unique ingredients, and special traditions make it stand out in a crowded field of superb Asian flavors.

With this book, you can explore the concepts and philosophy behind the ways in which traditional Korean cooking employs its various ingredients and techniques. The idea of yin and yang—that is, balance—is very important to a Korean meal, as well as an emphasis on the five basic elements of taste: salty, sweet, sour, spicy, and bitter. In addition, the book contains explanations of basic Korean pantry staples and kitchen tools and how to use them, followed by a variety of recipes to get you started in exploring the wonderful flavors of this increasingly popular cuisine. Mashikeh-mogoseyo! Bon appetit, the Korean way!

Introduction to Korean Cuisine

Note on transliterations: Korean identifiers for items and dishes are used throughout the book with English explanation. This cookbook adheres to the Revised Romanization transliteration (though spellings can sometimes vary: "gochugaru," for example, is sometimes rendered "kochukaru").

Location: Where Korean Cooking Comes From

Warm and sustaining may be the best two words to describe the experience of eating a Korean meal. As with many great world cuisines, what Koreans typically eat is the result of geography and climate: the Korean peninsula has a climate that is similar to the North Central part of the United States, which means that there are cold winters, warm, occasionally hot summers, and extended cool autumns. This allows for a growing season wherein many varieties of vegetables and grains can be cultivated.

The very cold winters also create the need for preservation. Before the 20th century, Korea was mainly a rural, agriculturally based society wherein foraging and farming were central to survival for most families. Hence the need to preserve the harvest throughout the winter, often in large earthenware pots buried in the ground. This is how something like the fermented cabbage dish kimchi, perhaps the most recognizable Korean product in the United States today, comes into the story. While kimchi is readily available in Asian markets and becoming more available in general grocery stores, it is surprisingly easy to make at home with excellent results. And kimchi is merely one of a whole host of preserved, pickled, or fermented foods that play a crucial role in the distinctive taste of Korean cuisine. What once began as necessity has, with time, become a treasured tradition and an indispensable ingredient in Korean cooking. It would be virtually unthinkable to conceive of a Korean cuisine without kimchi and its siblings. See Chapter 6 for a basic kimchi recipe, as well as some other varieties of common Korean style pickles.

The agricultural traditions of Korea also give rise to the creation of hearty, robust food, food that will sustain a farmer through a long day of work in the fields or the barns and guard against the elements. Warm spices and hot chilis are ubiquitous in Korean cooking, and hearty meals include not only a main dish and rice but also numerous small plates of various foods meant to be shared (collectively called **banchan**).

See Chapter 5 for further descriptions of and recipes for typical banchan.

Korean geography also plays a key role in the development of traditional cuisine. As it is mostly surrounded by bodies of water—the Yellow Sea to the east and the Sea of Japan to the west—seafood of various kinds feature significantly in Korean food, including fish (different to each coast), shellfish, and seaweeds. Here, yet again, the tradition of preservation plays an important role in the flavors of Korean food, as many types of seafood are dried or fermented for prolonged storage. And, as with kimchi, what was once the necessity of preservation has evolved into a beloved category of foodstuffs without which Korean food would not seem quite right. Dried sardines are served at nearly every meal, usually as a condiment to add a flavor punch of salt and funk. Dried cuttlefish is an immensely popular snack in Korea, found even in vending machines.

As you will see, the cuisine of Korea is undoubtedly unique, with its emphasis on bold flavors, hot chilis, and many styles of kimchi, with long-held traditions of sharing and respect around the table.

Yin and Yang: A Philosophy of Balance

The concept of yin and yang is familiar to almost anyone with a passing knowledge of Asian cultures. While many might immediately associate this concept with Chinese society, it is deeply ingrained within Korean culture, as well, and guides the principles of how to create a traditional Korean dish and meal.

"Yin" is associated with cooling, fresh foods, such as green vegetables and light dairy products (milk, yogurt, light cheeses). "Yang" is associated with warming, spicy foods, such as meat, chilis, and heavier dairy products. Yin food refreshes and relaxes the body, while yang food invigorates and makes the body strong. There are also "neutral" foods, as well, used to bring the yin and yang into balance. These foods provide stability and are relatively mild in taste, such as cereal grains and rice.

Cooking methods are also considered under the umbrella of "yin" or "yang." Grilling and frying, for example, are considered very "yang" ways of cooking, while poaching and steaming are typical "yin" in preparation. Foods that are left raw or fermented are also considered yin.

The idea is to create a meal that brings yin and yang into balance, with neutral foods to bind everything together. Thus, you have grilled meat, such as bulgogi (see Chapter 4 for a recipe) with some vegetable banchan (Chapter 5), fermented kimchi (Chapter 6), and rice. This balance in the meal is important in maintaining balance and health in the body, as Koreans believe, and thus eating becomes not only an act of sustenance but also an act of health and well-being.

Five Elements: Harmony of Flavors

Korean cooks also place an emphasis on utilizing and harmonizing the five basic elements of taste in their cooking: salty, sweet, sour, spicy, and bitter. This is also crucial to health, in that these five tastes in harmony can impact our organs and metabolism in positive ways. Traditional medicine often employs these concepts in nursing a person back to health, by prescribing certain foods and herbs that will assist the regeneration of certain organs (sour foods help the liver, it is thought, while bitter foods are good for the heart).

Take basic kimchi as an example. The sweetness and slight bitterness of fresh cabbage is salted to preserve it, usually with the addition of hot chili powder (gochugaru), and left to ferment creating a sour flavor. All five elements of taste are represented in this one dish, and as such, it has surely become the most renowned and ubiquitous Korean culinary creation.

Again, eating is more than simply to consume food out of necessity. Sitting down to a Korean meal is to engage in a sensory experience of all five elemental tastes, in harmony with the concept of yin and yang, with respect to traditional ideals of hospitality, generosity, and community.

The Korean Pantry

Below you will find a list of the most common ingredients used in traditional Korean cooking. Some of them will be familiar, while others may be new to you. For ingredients not found easily in the grocery store, try your local Asian market. Included are some suggestions for substitutions, but almost always, seeking out traditional ingredients is well worth the time and effort.

Gochugaru (Korean Chili Powder)

Gochugaru (sometimes spelled kochukaru) is the hot chili powder that is used frequently in Korean cooking. Made from dried red chilis, it is an essential pantry ingredient, especially important to kimchi. Other red chili powders can be substituted, but it must be noted that consistencies of chili powders vary widely (gochugaru is more a flake than a powder), so measurements will need to be adjusted accordingly, and the flavor will not be quite the same. Also beware of substituting American-style "chili powder," which often contains other spices in addition to the chili.

Gochujang (Korean Chili Paste)

This excellent, slightly sweet and not too spicy paste can be found at many Asian groceries and is used in a number of Korean dishes. Again, it is well worth seeking out, though it can be made at home with a few simple ingredients if you have some gochugaru on hand. This quick recipe will keep in your refrigerator for a month or more and is great to have on hand for any number of uses (tasty on most grilled foods, for example).

Method

Simply blend (in a food processor or blender) 2 tbsp of gochugaru, 2 trimmed and chopped scallions, toasted sesame oil, toasted and ground sesame seeds (2 tsps each), some minced garlic cloves, 2 tbsp of soy sauce, and a pinch of sugar, store in a container with a tightly fitted lid.

Doenjang (Fermented Soybean Paste)

This paste is made entirely from fermented soybeans and brine. Its cousin, Japanese miso, is also based on fermented soybeans but with the addition of a koji (rice) starter. Thus, doenjang is stronger in flavor in accordance with the more assertive flavors of traditional Korean cuisine.

Ganjang (Soy Sauce)

Most American home cooks are well acquainted with soy sauce. Korean soy sauce is similar to the Japanese variety most of us have in our cupboards. Koreans also use Guk-ganjang or "soup soy sauce" which is lighter and color and milder in flavor. Be aware that soy sauces with the label "naturally brewed" are typically superior products.

Chamgireum (Toasted Sesame Oil)

Toasted sesame oil is an indispensable ingredient for any well-stocked pantry, especially for the home cook interested in Asian food. Be aware that *toasted* sesame oil is a very different product than the sesame oil you find in the aisle next to other vegetable-based oils. Toasted sesame oil is a dark amber color with a deep nutty aroma. It is most often used at the end of the cooking process lest its deep flavors are lost.

Aekjeot (Fish Sauce)

Aekjeot (fish sauce) is part of a larger group of Korean pantry staples called jeotgal, which essentially means "salted seafood."Aekjeot is commonly used to kick off the fermentation process in kimchi as well as to season various soups and stews. Also widely used in Vietnamese and Thai cooking, brands from all countries can be found in Asian groceries.

Cheongju (Rice Wine)

Korean rice wine is often used in cooking, particularly in marinades and sometimes in sauces. It is a clear alcoholic beverage with a bit of sweetness to it. Japanese sake and Chinese Shaoxing are similar products; though do not make the mistake of substituting Japanese mirin for cheongju as it is a much sweeter product. Also, be sure to use actual rice wine and not the "cooking wine" that can often be found in supermarkets; "cooking wine" is often heavily salted or otherwise diluted in order to make it legal to sell to the general public.

Ssalsikcho (Rice Wine Vinegar)

Rice wine vinegar is useful to have on hand not only for Korean cooking but also for many other kinds of cooking. It is excellent in vinaigrettes, lighter than red or white wine vinegar, and can also be used in a wide variety of marinades and sauces. Rice wine and rice wine vinegar are *not* the same product: to boil it down simply, rice wine contains alcohol and rice wine vinegar does not. And, while rice wine vinegar is less tart than its Western counterparts, it is still tarter and less sweet than rice wine.

Kkae (Toasted Sesame Seeds)

Sesame seeds can be found already toasted in many Asian markets, sometimes already toasted and ground. But you can toast and/or grind sesame seeds at home with little fuss. To toast seeds, simply heat a small pan (medium-high) and swirl untoasted white sesame seeds for about three to five minutes until they turn a light brown. If you have an electric coffee grinder, you can also grind toasted or untoasted seeds into a powder when necessary for a recipe: just be sure to clean out the grinder well before and after each different use. Or, you can invest in a separate small grinder for seeds and other whole spices.

Chapsal (Glutinous or Sweet Rice Flour)

Sweet rice flour is used in many Asian cuisines, usually in desserts. Doughs made from glutinous rice flour are sticky and elastic and have a unique mouthfeel.

See Chapter 8 for Korean desserts using this product.

Korean Kitchen Tools

To cook good quality Korean food, the average home cook will need only to utilize whatever tools she or he already has in the cupboard. However, it is worth exploring some of the kitchen tools unique to Korean cooking and serving. These bowls and pots and utensils are indicative of Korean tradition, reminding the chef and the guest of earth and stone, of the natural world from which the elements of food and culture emanate.

Dolsot (Stone Bowl)

The dolsot is a stone bowl used both for cooking and serving. As much of Korean cooking is hearty and unpretentious, so is the dolsot. Often used in dolsot bibimbap (see Chapter 4 for a recipe), the stone can get so hot that it can essentially fry an egg or crisp cooked rice.

Onggi (Clay Pot)

These lovely clay pots are used both for serving and for storage. Large onggi are traditionally used in kimchi making, wherein the prepared kimchi is packed into the pot and buried in the ground to ferment. Onggi allows the bubbles created by fermentation to escape through its porous structure while keeping the food within fresh and free of spoilage. Until recent years, you could find buried crocks of onggi scattered throughout the countryside in Korea, and they still remain valuable and beautiful serving and storage vessels.

Siru (Earthenware Steamer)

As with the above dolsot and onggi, the siru is also a product of the earth, made with glazed and unglazed clay. It is a steamer for rice cakes and rice flour dishes, such as tteok (see Chapter 8). Historically, the siru was also used in ritual preparations of dishes for different celebrations.

Sujeo (Utensils)

This term refers collectively to the long-handled metal spoon and metal chopsticks used at nearly every Korean meal. Often, the sujeo set is carved with symbolic scenes of natural beauty, and elaborately carved sets were traditionally presented as wedding gifts. For those accustomed to eating with Chinese or Japanese style wooden or lacquered chopsticks, using the flatter metal chopsticks of Korea are a challenge initially, but their distinctive style and beauty make the effort worth the while.

Tabletop Grill

While not essential for making great Korean barbecue, the tabletop grill is a fun, innovative, and ultimately practical manner of cooking marinated cuts of meat and vegetables to order. Each diner can modify the cooking time according to his or her tastes, and the act of participating is quite enjoyable—not to mention the wonderful aromas that waft through the dining room. This method of cooking is so popular in Korea that many restaurant dining tables have grills built into the table itself. In the United States, it has become increasingly easy to find Korean restaurants who offer this kind of cooking via a portable tabletop grill, and a home cook interested in diving into the glories of Korean grilling would make great use of such a specialty tool. Bulgogi and galbi are two popular dishes that are often prepared this way (see Chapter 4 for recipes).

Rice Cooker

Most home cooks are familiar with the rice cooker. They are handy to have around not just for rice but also for steaming vegetables, dumplings, and in the case of Korean cooking, some tteok desserts. There are numerous cookers from which to choose; from expensive models that can automatically turn themselves off when sensors detect the rice is perfectly cooked to economical models that do the job well if simply. An inexpensive rice cooker is a good investment for the industrious home cook.

Korean Staples: Recipes & Guidelines for Common Dishes

Bap (Rice)

A Korean meal would hardly be Korean without rice. This staple is omnipresent, both as a simple side and as a building block for other main courses. Below are some simple recipes for Korean style rice and its many iterations.

- Prep & Cook Time: 25 min. (plus soaking, optional)
- Yield: 6 servings

Nutrition Info per serving

- Calories 225
- Fat 0g
- Carbohydrates 49.3g
- Sodium 3mg

Ingredients

- 2 cups short grain rice

Preparation

1. Wash and rinse rice in a saucepan, swishing it around in the water to release starch, at least three times. Drain.
2. Put 2 ½ cups water in a pan with rice and, if you like, soak for about half an hour before cooking (this helps rice to cook evenly and quickly).
3. Heat pan on medium-high temp, let it boil, then cover. Switch to low temp. Let rice steam for 15 minutes without removing the cover. Remove from heat, let rice stand for another 5 minutes without removing the cover. Fluff and serve.

Gukbap (Rice Soup)

Essentially, there are limitless varieties of gukbap; any soup that contains rice is a kind of gukbap. One of the most common is with bean sprouts (see below), but also visit Chapter 7 for other soups, almost all of which could benefit from a scoop of rice.

- Prep & Cook Time: 20 min
- Yield: 4-5 servings

Nutrition Info per serving

- Calories 403
- Fat 4.7g
- Carbohydrates 58g
- Sodium 1240mg

Ingredients

- 6 cups stock
- 2 cloves garlic, minced
- 2 tsps gochugaru
- 1 package bean sprouts (12 ounces)
- 2 cups cooked rice
- 1 cup chopped kimchi
- A couple of tsps sesame seeds
- 2 tsps toasted sesame oil
- 2 green onions, sliced

Preparation

1. Heat stock with garlic and gochugaru while you ready rest of ingredients. Blanch the bean sprouts boiling salted-water for 4 or 5 minutes then drain.
2. Divide rice, kimchi, and sprouts among 4
3. heatproof bowls, pour a little sesame oil and a sprinkling of green onions and sesame seeds. If you like, nest an egg yolk in the center of each bowl. Pour hot broth over each serving.

Juk (Rice Porridge)

Like gukbap, juk takes well to any number of ingredients (see Chapter 7 for a seafood version): a handful of chopped kimchi or other pickles; broiled or grilled meat; an egg yolk or fried egg. Below is a basic version of porridge to get started.

- Prep & Cook Time: 35 min. plus overnight soaking
- Yield: 4 servings

Nutrition Info per serving

- Calories 225
- Fat 0g
- Carbohydrates 49.3g
- Sodium 3 mg

Ingredients

- 2 cups short grain rice

Preparation

1. Wash rice in a few (3 or 4) changes of water, swirling rice around until water becomes clear. Drain a final time and add 4 cups of water to rice. Leave to soak overnight.
2. Drain rice again, and then add to saucepan with additional water (6 cups). Let it boil, put a lid, and put on medium-low. Let cook for a good 30 minutes. Serve with toppings and seasonings as desired.

Bokkeum-bap (Fried Rice 1)

- Prep & Cook Time: 25 min.
- Yield: 4-5 servings

Nutrition Info per serving

- Calories 726
- Fat 12.2g
- Carbohydrates 126g
- Sodium 525mg

Ingredients

- 3 cups cooked rice
- 2 tbsps neutral oil
- ½ small onion or 1 shallot, finely chopped
- 2-3 minced cloves garlic
- ¾ pound ground beef, chicken, or pork
- 1/3 cup kimchi, chopped
- 3 cups mixed vegetables (zucchini, bell pepper, carrot, snap peas), chopped
- Oyster sauce (about 2 tbsps)
- Toasted sesame oil (about 2 tsps)
- 2 scallions, sliced
- 1 or 2 fried eggs (optional)

Preparation

1. Have all the ingredients ready before starting. Heat the oil on medium-high in a large skillet, add garlic, onion and stir fry until slightly colored, 2-3 minutes. Add meat and stir fry until browned, about 5-6 minutes.
2. Add kimchi as well as vegetables and stir fry for another 5 minutes. Add rice then mix everything together, cooking 5 more minutes.
3. Drizzle with oyster sauce and sesame oil, and transfer to a platter. Scatter scallions over and top with a fried egg or two, if using.

Mushroom Rice

- Prep & Cook Time: 45 minutes or so
- Yield: 4-6 servings

Nutrition Info per serving

- Calories 233
- Fat 8.6g
- Carbohydrates 23.6g
- Sodium 329mg

Ingredients

- Full 2 cups rice, short grain
- Neutral oil, about 2 tbsps
- 1 white or yellow onion, chopped
- ½ pound mushrooms, sliced
- ½ pound ground beef or pork
- 1 tsp toasted sesame oil
- 2 tbsps soy sauce
- 2 tsps sesame seeds
- 2 scallions, sliced

Preparation:

1. Wash rice 2 or 3 times, then cover with water to soak while preparing rest of ingredients. Over medium-high heat, put oil in large skillet, then cook onion until softened,

about 5-7 minutes. Add mushrooms and meat, making sure to break up any clumps of meat, until browned, 10 minutes.
2. Drain rice and put in skillet, accompanied by enough water to cover by ½ inch (about 3 cups). Let this simmer for 15 minutes, then test rice for doneness. If it needs more cooking time and/or more water, adjust as necessary.
3. When rice is cooked, add soy, sesame oil, and seeds, then garnish with scallions.

Bibimbap (Rice Dish with Meat and Vegetables)

This dish is perhaps one of the best known Korean dishes. It is highly versatile and an excellent platform for using leftover rice, bulgogi, and banchan.

- Prep & Cook Time: 30 minutes
- Yield: 4 servings

Nutrition Info per serving

- Calories 878
- Fat 27g
- Carbohydrates 117 g
- Sodium 615 mg

Ingredients

- ½ pound ground or thinly sliced beef
- 2 tbsps soy sauce
- 2 cloves of garlic; minced
- 3 tbsps sesame oil, toasted and divided
- 1 tbsp plus 1 tsp sugar, divided
- 1 ½ or 2 tbsps gochujang
- 2 tsps rice wine vinegar
- 1 tbsp sesame seeds
- 2 tbsps neutral oil
- ½ cup spinach
- ½ cup shitake mushrooms, chopped
- ¾ cup bean sprouts
- 3 cups cooked rice
- 4 fried eggs
- Toasted seaweed (nori), for garnish

Preparation

1. Marinate the beef in all of the soy sauce, 2 tbsps sesame oil, garlic and 1 tsp of the sugar while you prepare other ingredients.
2. Make the sauce with gochujang, rice wine vinegar, sesame seeds, and remaining sesame oil and sugar.

3. Heat neutral oil in large saute pan, then cook beef until browned, around 5-6 minutes. Add spinach, mushrooms, and bean sprouts, and then stir fry until all ingredients are cooked. (A note here: oftentimes, bibimbap is presented with each ingredient separate, as opposed to tossing together; this takes longer but makes for a prettier presentation, if desired.)
4. Mix in sauce, then divide rice among bowls, top with meat and vegetable mixture, place a fried egg on top of each serving and, if you like, garnish with nori.

Tteok-bokki (Spicy Rice Cakes)

- Prep & Cook Time: About an hour
- Yield: 2-3 servings

Nutrition Info per serving

Calories 478

Fat 3.6 g

Carbohydrates 100 g

Sodium 1175 mg

Ingredients

- 1 pound rice cakes
- 3 cups stock or water
- 3 tbsps gochujang
- 2-3 tsps gochugaru
- 1 tbsp soy sauce

- 3-4 minced cloves of garlic
- 2 tbsps sugar
- ¼ pound Korean fish cake (available in Asian markets), chopped into ½ pieces
- ½ cup chopped Napa cabbage
- 2 scallions, sliced

Preparation

1. Soak rice cakes for 20 minutes. Meanwhile, heat stock while making the sauce. Stir together gochujang, soy, sugar, and garlic for the sauce.
2. Add sauce to stock and bring to a boil. Put rice cakes into the sauce and simmer for around 20 minutes, until cooked through.
3. Add fish cakes and cabbage and cook another 5 minutes, or until fish cakes are softened. Serve hot, garnished with scallions.

BibimGuksu (Spicy Noodle Dish)

- Prep & Cook Time: 30 minutes
- 4 servings

Nutrition Info per serving

- Calories 418
- Fat 9.4 g
- Carbohydrates 66 g
- Sodium 146 mg

Ingredients

- 1 cup kimchi, chopped
- ½ cup kimchi liquid
- 1/3 cup gochujang
- 2 tsps sugar
- 3 tsps rice wine vinegar
- 1 tbsp sesame seeds
- 1 tbsp toasted sesame oil
- 1 pound somyeon (thin wheat-based noodles)
- 1 cup cucumber, julienned
- 2 hardboiled eggs

Preparation

1. Mix all ingredients up to noodles. Taste and adjust for seasonings.

2. Meanwhile, in a large pot, let water boil. Add noodles; cook until done, about 8-9 minutes. Strain then rinse under cold water, to keep noodles from sticking together. Toss with chunky sauce mixture, distribute among bowls, with ¼ cup cucumber and half a hardboiled egg on top. Serve immediately or noodles lose their texture.

Japchae (Glass Noodle Stir Fry)

- Prep & Cook Time: 45-50minuntes
- 4 servings

Nutrition Info per serving

- Calories 388
- Fat 20 g
- Carbohydrates 40 g
- Sodium 1014 mg

Ingredients

- 6 dried shitake mushrooms, soaked
- ½ pound spinach
- 3 tbsps soy sauce
- 4 cloves of minced garlic
- 2 tbsps sugar
- 2 tbsps sesame seeds
- 1-2 tbsps toasted sesame oil
- ¼ pound thinly sliced beef
- 6 ounces dangmyeon (sweet potato or starch noodles)
- 2 ½ tbsps neutral oil
- 1 carrot, julienned
- 1 small white onion, diced
- 2 scallions, chopped

Preparation

1. Soak mushrooms for 20 minutes, then stem and slice caps. In boiling water, blanch spinach for 45 seconds, then drain, let cool, and squeeze dry. Coarsely chop.
2. Make the sauce by mixing soy, sugar, garlic, sesame oil and seeds. Toss beef with 1 tbsp of sauce; toss mushrooms with 1 tbsp of sauce. Put 2 tbsps of sauce in large bowl and reserve.
3. Cook noodles in a pan of boiling water until done, about 7-8 minutes. Put in a strainer, sluice with cold water, and drain again.
4. Heat ½ tbsp oil over medium-high heat in large skillet, then stir fry noodles for 3 minutes. Transfer to bowl with reserved sauce.
5. Heat part of neutral oil in the same pan and stir fry carrot, scallion, and onion until not quite soft, about 4 minutes. Place in a bowl with noodles.
6. Heat remaining oil and saute beef and mushrooms until slightly browned for 3-4 minutes. Place in a bowl with noodles and vegetables. Add blanched spinach and toss well, incorporating and adding more sauce to taste.

MulNaengmyeon (Cold Noodle Soup)

- Prep & Cook Time: 40 minutes
- For 2 servings

Nutrition Info per serving

- Fat 4 g
- Calories 288
- Carbohydrates 46 g
- Sodium 3170 mg

Ingredients

- 1 daikon radish
- 2 tbsps salt
- 2 tbsps sugar
- 5 tbsps rice wine vinegar, divided
- 2 cups beef broth
- 2 cups chicken broth
- ¼ pound naengmyeon noodles (buckwheat noodles)
- 1 Asian pear, julienned
- ½ cup julienned cucumber
- 1 hardboiled egg, halved
- Sliced brisket or chicken (optional)

Preparation

1. Make radish pickle: cut daikon into ½ inch pieces, then mix with salt, sugar, and 2 tbsps vinegar. Set aside for at least 15 minutes.
2. Mix both broths with remaining 3 tbsps vinegar and put in the fridge for a good 30 minutes to chill.
3. Cook noodles in boiling water until toothsome, 5 minutes or so. Place in strainer and wash with cold water.
4. Divide noodles and broth in bowls, then top with pear, cucumber, and egg, and some reserved radish pickle

(about 2 tbsps per serving; reserve remaining pickle for another use). If you have prepared the chicken or beef broth yourself, divide some leftover meat from cooking broth among bowls, as well.

Mandu (Dumplings 1)

- Prep & Cook Time: 1 hour
- Yield: 40 dumplings

Nutrition Info per serving

- Calories 453 |
- Fat 10 g
- Carbohydrates 53 g
- Sodium 806 mg

Ingredients

- 1/2 pound zucchini, finely diced
- 10 ounces Napa cabbage, finely chopped
- ¼ pound mushrooms, finely chopped
- ½ white or yellow onion, finely diced
- 8 ounces ground pork

- 4 ounces ground beef
- 3 cloves garlic, minced
- 2 tsps ginger, grated
- 1 tbsp toasted sesame oil
- 1 tbsp soy sauce
- 1 large egg
- 1 package mandu (dumpling) wrappers (about 40)

For Dipping Sauce:
- 1 tbsp water
- 1 tbsp soy sauce
- 1 tsp of rice wine vinegar
- Scant tsp gochugaru
- ½ tsp sugar

Preparation

1. Place zucchini and cabbage into 2 separate bowls or strainers and toss generously with salt. Let sit for at least 15 minutes, then wring out excess liquid and place together in one large bowl.
2. Put everything else except wrappers into a bowl and mix together well, seasoning with a little salt and pepper as needed (about ¼ tsp of each).
3. In the middle of the wrapper, put a heaped tsp of filling, then wet one edge and fold into a crescent shape, pressing to seal edges. You can plait edges, if you like, or crimp with

a fork, but this is not required. Just be sure the dumplings are sealed. Repeat until all filling and wrappers are used. (Dumplings can be frozen at this point: put on cookie sheets and freeze for an hour, then put into freezer bags for up to 2 months. No need to thaw before cooking, just add a couple of minutes to total cooking time.)
4. Make the dipping sauce by mixing all ingredients together.
5. Cook dumplings using one of the following methods:

   A. **Pan Fry**: in batches over medium-high, heat 1 tbsp neutral oil, then add about 8 dumplings, making sure they don't touch. Brown for 2 minutes, add 1/3 cup water and cover, steaming dumplings for an additional 5 minutes.
   B. **Deep Fry**: pour neutral oil (about 3 inches deep) in a large pan and get the temperature to 350 degrees. Fry dumplings in batches, about 3 minutes.
   C. **Steam**: Line steamer basket with cabbage leaves and steam dumplings in batches for 10 minutes. Again, be sure they don't touch or they might stick together.
   D. **Boil:** Cook in boiling water in batches until dumplings float, then continue to cook for about 2 minutes.

Kimchi Mandu (Dumplings 2)

Follow the cooking methods for the previous recipe to make these dumplings. Easy to make if you have prepared kimchi on hand (see Chapter 6 for recipe).

- Prep & Cook Time: 1 hour
- Yield: 25 dumplings

Nutrition Info per serving

- Calories 396
- Fat 10.6 g
- Carbohydrates 46 g
- Sodium 615 mg

Ingredients

- 1 ½ cups kimchi, finely chopped
- ½ pound firm tofu, finely chopped
- ½ pound bean sprouts, blanched and finely chopped
- ¼ pound ground pork or beef
- 6 scallions, finely chopped
- 1 large egg
- 2 tsps toasted sesame oil
- ¼ tsp each salt and pepper
- About 25 mandu (dumpling) wrappers

Preparation

1. Mix all ingredients, except wrappers, together. Fill and cook dumplings as directed in the above recipe, Mandu (Dumplings 1).

Bulgogi (Grilled Beef)

- Prep & Cook Time:15 min. plus 8 hours marinating time
- Yield: 6 servings

Nutrition Info per serving

- Calories 468
- Fat 25.5 g
- Carbohydrates 12.5 g
- Sodium 1288 mg

Ingredients

- 1 Asian pear, peeled
- 2 cloves garlic
- ½ cup of soy sauce
- ¼ gochugaru
- Toasted sesame oil, 1-2 tbsps
- 2 tbsps chopped ginger
- 2 tbsps sugar
- 2 lbs. beef tenderloin
- 2 scallions, sliced, for garnish
- 1-2 tbsps neutral oil (optional, if pan frying)

Preparation

1. Put all ingredients excepting beef in a food processor or blender and puree. Thinly slice beef and coat with marinade. (If you freeze the beef for about 30 minutes

before slicing, it is easier to make neat, thin slices.) Refrigerate in the marinade for 8 hours to overnight.
2. Traditionally, bulgogi is grilled, either tableside or outdoors; however, it can be cooked over high heat in a large skillet in 2 or 3 batches, about 5 minutes per batch. Garnish with scallions.

Bulgogi Sauce

This is a nice addition to any grilled meat.

Simply mix together:

- 2 tbsps water,
- ¼ soy sauce,
- 1 tbsp each of rice wine vinegar and chopped scallions,
- 1 minced garlic clove,
- 2 tsps gochujang,
- 1 tsp sesame seeds (ground for a smoother sauce, if you like).

Daweaji Bulgogi (Grilled Pork)

- Prep & Cook Time: 20 minutes, plus 1 hour marinating time
- Yield: 4 servings

Nutrition Info per serving

- Calories 469
- Fat 27.7 g
- Carbohydrates 14.2 g
- Sodium 921mg

Ingredients

- 3 tbsps gochujang
- 1 tbsp gochugaru
- 2 tbsps soy sauce
- 2 tbsps rice wine vinegar

- 1 tbsp sesame oil
- 1 tbsp sugar
- 3 cloves garlic, minced
- 1 tbsp ginger, grated
- 1 pound pork shoulder or belly
- ½ white onion, sliced thinly
- 3 scallions, chopped
- 1 tbsp neutral oil (optional, for pan frying)

Preparation

1. Combine all ingredients up to pork for the marinade. Thinly slice pork (place in freezer for 30 minutes before slicing for easier, neater slices) and coat with marinade. Toss in onion and scallions. Leave in marinade for at least an hour at room temperature or 4 hours refrigerated.
2. Cook over high heat on a grill until caramelized and cooked completely. Alternately, heat neutral oil over medium-high in a large skillet and pan fry until done, 5-6 minutes.

Dak Bulgogi (Grilled Chicken 1)

- Prep & Cook Time: 25 min. plus 1 hour marinating time
- Yield: 4 servings

Nutrition Info per serving

- Calories 286
- Fat 8 g
- Carbohydrates 13.3 g
- Sodium 991 mg

Ingredients

- 4 tbsps soy sauce
- 2 tbsps lemon juice
- 2 tbsps sugar
- 1 tbsp honey
- 1 tbsp toasted sesame oil
- 1 tbsp rice wine vinegar
- 3 cloves garlic, minced
- 2 tsps grated ginger
- 1 tsp sesame seeds
- 1 ½ pounds chicken thighs or breasts (skinless, boneless)
- 2 scallions, sliced, for garnish
- 2 tbsps neutral oil (optional, if pan frying)

Preparation

1. Mix together all ingredients except chicken. Cut chicken into ½ inch pieces and toss with marinade. Let marinate in the fridge for an hour.
2. Grill or cook over medium-high heat in a large skillet, roughly 2 minutes a side. Be careful here, as the sugar and honey can easily burn. Garnish with scallions.

Dak Bulgogi (Grilled Chicken 2)

- Preparation& Cooking Time: 40 min. plus overnight marinating
- For 4 servings

Nutrition Info per serving

- Calories 678
- Fat 46 g
- Carbohydrates 11.5 g
- Sodium 1416 mg

Ingredients

- ¼ cup sesame seeds, toasted
- 5 minced garlic cloves
- 1 tbsp grated ginger
- ¼ cup of soy sauce
- 2 tbsps sugar
- 2 tbsps toasted sesame oil
- ½ tsp salt
- Gochugaru (optional, for a spicier version, 2 or 3 tsps)
- 1 3-4 chicken, cut into 10 serving pieces (2 wings, 2 breasts cut in half, 2 thighs, 2 legs)
- 3 scallions, sliced, for garnish

Preparation

1. Grind half of the sesame seeds (set the whole seeds aside for garnish), then combine with everything except chicken and scallions. Stir in the ¼ cup of water and mix well.
2. Make 2 slashes in each chicken piece to allow for the marinade to penetrate, then cover with marinade and refrigerate overnight.
3. Grill over moderate heat for about 30 minutes, until charred and cooked through. Turn frequently to prevent burning and watch for flare-ups. Alternately, roast the chicken in for thirty minutes at 450 degrees, turning once. Garnish with scallion and reserved sesame seeds.

Galbi (Grilled Short Ribs)

- Preparation& Cooking Time:20 minutes plus overnight marinating
- For 4 servings

Nutrition Info per serving

- Calories 1157
- Fat 47 g
- Carbohydrates 42 g
- Sodium 2200 mg

Ingredients

- ½ cup of water
- ½ cup of soy sauce
- ¼ cup of rice wine
- ¼ cup of sugar
- 1 Asian pear, peeled

- ½ onion
- 3 scallions
- 5 minced cloves garlic
- 1 tsp grated ginger
- 2 tbsps honey
- 2 tbsps toasted sesame oil
- 4 pounds beef short ribs, flanken cut (across the bone)
- Sliced scallions and sesame seeds, for garnish

Preparation

1. Put everything except ribs and garnish in a food processor or blender and roughly puree. Pound ribs to tenderize (optional), then cover with marinade and refrigerate overnight.
2. Grill until caramelized and cooked thoroughly, over high heat, about 3 minutes a side. Alternately, you can broil ribs under a preheated broiler for roughly 5 minutes a side. Garnish with scallions and sesame seeds.

Mulgogi Gochujang (Spicy Fish)

- Prep & Cooking Time: 30 min.
- For 4 servings

Nutrition Info per serving

- Carbohydrates 21.8 g
- Sodium 1065 mg
- Calories 269
- Fat 14.6g

Ingredients

- 1 tbsp gochujang
- 1 tbsp sugar
- 2 tbsps soy sauce
- 1 tbsp toasted sesame oil
- 2 cloves garlic, minced
- 4 fish fillets (mackerel, bluefish, preferably skin on)
- Garnishes: sliced scallions and sesame seeds

Preparation

1. Mix everything except fish together, and rub all over fish. Preheat broiler and place fish, skin side down on oiled foil placed in broiling pan (for easier clean up).
2. Broil until top is browned, keeping fish around 6 inches from element, about 8 minutes. Check for doneness but beware of overcooking. Garnish with scallions and sesame seeds.

Kkanpung Saeu (Spicy and Sweet Shrimp)

- Prep & Cook Time: 1 hour
- Yield: 4 servings

Nutrition Info per serving

- Calories 560
- Fat 5.9 g
- Carbohydrates 95.5 g
- Sodium 306 mg

Ingredients

For sauce:

- 2 tbsps each:
- Soy sauce
- Oyster sauce
- Sugar
- Rice wine vinegar
- Rice wine
- Broth (chicken or anchovy stock) or water
- 1 tbsp lemon juice

For stir fry:

- 1 pound shrimp, peeled
- 8 tbsps potato starch
- 1 large egg
- Neutral oil, for frying
- 4 dried red peppers, broken into pieces
- 5 cloves garlic, sliced thinly
- 1-inch piece of ginger, julienned
- 1 scallion, sliced
- ¼ white onion, thinly sliced
- ¼ bell pepper (any color), finely diced
- 1 mild green chili pepper (such as Anaheim), finely diced
- ½ tbsp toasted sesame oil, for drizzling

Preparation

1. Mix all of the sauce ingredients; set this aside as you prepare shrimp.
2. Devein shrimp, if you like, and mix potato starch with egg, then coat shrimp with batter. Heat enough oil in large pan to fry shrimp, in batches if necessary, and fry coated shrimp until crispy and browned, about 3 minutes per batch. Place on paper towels to catch excess oil and reserve.

3. Heat about a tbsp of oil in large pan, and then add aromatics: dried peppers, garlic, ginger, scallion, onion, bell pepper, and green pepper. Over high heat, stir fry for 3-4 minutes. Pour in sauce and bring to a boil. Cook for an additional 2-3 minutes until sauce thickens slightly. Add reserved shrimp and toss everything together well. Serve immediately, drizzled with sesame oil.

Banchan: Shared Small Dishes for Every Meal

Banchan refers to the series of small side dishes that are served with virtually every meal around a Korean table. These dishes are all meant to be shared, with a few bites of many different varieties for everyone. The more formal the meal, the more banchan will be served, typically. The following are some quick and easy recipes for Korean banchan that you can serve at home. Most banchan can be served at room temperature.

All of the following recipes serve about 4 people with a main dish or stew and white rice unless otherwise noted.

Bokkeum: Stir-Fried Dishes

Hobak Bokkeum (Stir-fried Zucchini)

- Prep & Cook Time: 15 min.

Nutrition Info per serving

- Calories 58
- Fat 5g
- Carbohydrates 2.8g
- Sodium 353mg

Ingredients

- 1 medium zucchini
- 1 tbsp neutral oil, such as canola
- 2 cloves of garlic, minced
- 3 tsps fish sauce
- 1 tsp toasted sesame oil
- 1 scallion, minced
- 1 tsp sesame seeds, preferably toasted

Preparation

1. Slice zucchini in half lengthwise, then in ¼ inch slices crosswise, to create half-moons.
2. Heat tbsp of oil over medium-high heat in saute pan. Toss in zucchini, garlic, and fish sauce and cook for 4 minutes.

3. Stir in the sesame oil, scallion, and 2 tbsps of water and continue cooking for another 2 minutes, until zucchini softens.
4. Sprinkle with sesame seeds and serve.

Oi Bokkeum (Stir-fried cucumbers)

- Prep & Cook Time: 20 min.

Nutrition Info per serving

- Calories 29
- Fat 5 g
- Carbohydrates 11 g
- Sodium 879mg

Ingredients

- 3 Kirby cucumbers or 1 English cucumber
- 1 ½ tsps salt
- 3 tsps neutral oil
- 1 minced clove garlic
- 1 minced scallion
- 1 tsp each of toasted sesame oil and sesame seeds

Preparation

1. Cut the cucumbers into half-moon shapes (no need to de-seed them if using Kirby or English cucumber). Toss with salt and let sit for at least 5 minutes in a strainer. Squeeze dry before continuing.
2. Heat neutral oil on medium-high temp, toss in cucumbers, garlic, and scallion and stir fry for 2 minutes.
3. Off heat, sprinkle with sesame oil and seeds.

Gaji Bokkeum (Stir-fried Eggplant)

- Prep & Cook Time: 15 min.

Nutrition Info per serving

- Calories 136
- Fat 10 g
- Carbohydrates 12 g
- Sodium 262 mg

Ingredients

- 2 medium Asian eggplants (small and slender, not large globe eggplants)
- 3 mild green chili peppers or half a green bell pepper
- 2 tbsps neutral oil
- ½ tbsp gochujang
- 1 tbsp rice wine
- 1 tbsp soy sauce
- 2 cloves garlic, minced
- 1 tsp. sugar
- 2 tsps toasted sesame oil
- 1 tsp. sesame seeds

Preparation

1. Cut eggplants into half moons and cut chili peppers into slim rounds (1/2 inch pieces if using bell pepper).

2. Heat oil (medium-high heat) in saucepan and add eggplant and peppers. Stir fry for 2 minutes, or until the eggplant softens, add all remaining ingredients except sesame oil and seeds. Stir fry until eggplant is cooked and the peppers wilt roughly 5 minutes.
3. Sprinkle with sesame oil and seeds and serve.

Myulchi Bokkeum (Stir-fried Anchovies)

- Prep & Cook Time: 20 min.

Nutrition Info per serving

- Calories 195
- Fat 18.8 g
- Carbohydrates 3,7 g
- Sodium 638 mg

Ingredients

- 1 cup dried anchovies
- 3 tbsps neutral oil
- 1 minced clove garlic
- 1 tbsp sugar
- 2 tbsps toasted sesame oil
- 2 tsps gochujang
- 1 tbsp soy sauce
- 1 tsp sesame seeds

Preparation

1. Soak anchovies in water for about 10 minutes.
2. Put oil in skillet and heat on medium. Drain and add anchovies to oil. Saute until browned and crisp, about 8 minutes.

3. Add rest of ingredients except sesame seeds and saute another 2 minutes for flavors to meld. Adjust seasonings to taste, then transfer anchovies to paper towels to drain and sprinkle with sesame seeds.

Buchimgaeor Jeon (Korean Pancakes)

The terms buchimgae and jeon refer to cooking a variety of ingredients in a pancake-like batter. These can be made with meat, seafood, or vegetables. Below are a few recipes for vegetable-centered buchimgae.

Kimchi Buchimgae (Kimchi Pancake)

- Prep & Cooking Time: 25 min.
- Yield: 4 large pancakes

Nutrition Info per serving

- Calories 166
- Fat 10 g
- Carbohydrates 31.9 g
- Sodium 352 mg

Ingredients

- 2 ½ cups each: all-purpose flour and water
- 1 large egg
- 2 cups kimchi, coarsely chopped
- 1 tbsp kimchi pickling liquid
- Some neutral oil
- 2 or 3 green or red chilis, sliced (optional)
- Sliced scallions for garnish

Preparation

1. Whisk together flour, water, and egg, then stir in kimchi and kimchi liquid to the mix. Throw in a few ice cubes to keep batter cold while heating pan.
2. Heat about 1 tbsp oil over high heat in a nonstick pan, then add ¼ of batter. Sprinkle chilis over, if using. Cook for about 1 minute, then place on medium-low heat and cook until bottom is done and edges start to cook about 4-5 minutes.
3. Flip pancake and cook another 4-5 minutes. Slide out of the pan, cut into wedges or squares and garnish with scallions. Repeat with remaining ingredients.

Pajeon (Scallion Pancake)

- Prep & Cook Time: 15 min.
- Yield: Makes 2 pancakes

Nutrition Info per serving

- Calories 242
- Fat 15 g
- Carbohydrates 22 g
- Sodium 307 mg

Ingredients

- ¾ cup each: all-purpose flour and ice water
- 2 tbsps cornstarch
- 1 minced clove garlic
- ½ tsp salt
- 1 lightly beaten egg
- 1 bunch scallions, trimmed, halved if thick
- 4 tbsps neutral oil

Preparation

1. Mix together flour, cornstarch, garlic, salt, ice water and half of the beaten egg. Thin the batter with some more water to create the consistency of thick cream, if necessary.

2. Heat 2 tbsps oil over medium heat in a nonstick pan, then pour half the batter into the pan and immediately lay half the scallions on top of the batter. Drizzle with half the remaining beaten egg and cook for 4 minutes.
3. Turn pancake over and cook for another 3-4 minutes. Repeat with remaining ingredients.

Hobak Buchimgae (Zucchini Pancakes)

- Prep & Cook Time: 30 min.
- Yields: 2 pancakes

Nutrition Info per serving

- Calories 191
- Fat 14 g
- Carbohydrates 14.7 g
- Sodium 50 mg

Ingredients

- 1 medium zucchini, cut into matchstick shapes
- Salt
- 1 shallot, thinly sliced
- 2 green chili peppers, such as serranos, thinly sliced and seeded
- 6 tbsps flour
- 2 tbsps cornstarch
- 1 large egg
- 4 tbsps neutral oil

Preparation

1. Toss the zucchini with about ½ tsp of salt and set aside in a bowl for 12 minutes. Squeeze well, reserving liquid in the bowl, and set zucchini aside.

2. Add flour, cornstarch, and egg to bowl with zucchini liquid and mix together well. Stir in the zucchini, shallot, and chili peppers. If the mixture is too thick, add another couple of tbsps of water.
3. Heat 2 tbsps oil over medium heat in nonstick pan. Spoon in half of the batter mixture and cook for about 5 minutes each side. Repeat with remaining oil and batter.

Gamja Jeon (Potato Pancakes)

- Prep & Cook Time: 30 min.
- Yields: 6 small pancakes

Nutrition Info per serving

- Calories 150
- Fat 11.7 g
- Carbohydrates 11 g
- Sodium 200 mg

Ingredients

- 2 medium baking potatoes, peeled
- ½ medium white or yellow onion, peeled
- ½ tsp salt
- 1 green chili pepper, sliced (optional)
- 1 scallion, sliced (optional)
- 4 tbsps neutral oil

Preparation

1. Puree the potatoes in a food processor or blender, then spoon into a strainer over a bowl and let sit for about 5 minutes.
2. Meanwhile, puree the onion and pour into another bowl, then add the strained potato to this with the salt.

3. Stir in reserved potato liquid until the mixture reaches a batter-like consistency.
4. Heat 2 tbsps oil in nonstick pan and make 3 small pancakes with half the batter. Top each with some sliced chili and/or scallion and cook for roughly 5 minutes a side, so the cake is browned and crisp. Repeat with remaining oil and batter.

Pancake Dipping Sauce

Korean pancakes are typically served with a basic soy dipping sauce. To make, combine equal parts soy sauce, water, and rice vinegar and half part sugar (so, for example, 4 tbsps soy, water, vinegar to 2 tbsps sugar). The sauce can be enhanced with any number of flavors should you wish to embellish: add some sliced scallion and/or minced garlic for pungency; thinly sliced green or red chili or some gochugaru for heat; and/or some toasted sesame oil or sesame seeds for nuttiness.

Namul (Vegetables)

This category of banchan side dishes broadly refers to fresh greens, vegetables, and herbs often made with seasonal ingredients.

While typically steamed or blanched before seasoning, namul can also be boiled or fried or served raw.

Below are some recipes for common namul dishes, but use your imagination and your own seasonal ingredients to tailor these recipes to your tastes and locale.

Kongnamul Muchim (Seasoned Bean Sprouts)

- Prep & Cook Time: 10 min.

Nutrition Info per serving

- Calories 72
- Fat 4 g
- Carbohydrates 5.9 g
- Sodium 590 mg

Ingredients

- 1 pound of bean sprouts
- 1 tsp salt
- 2 minced scallions
- 2 minced cloves garlic
- 1 tbsp toasted sesame oil
- 1 tsp.sesame seeds
- Salt to taste
- 1-2 tsps gochugaru (optional, for a spicier version)
- 1 tbsp soy sauce (optional, for a spicier version)

Preparation:

1. Make sure sprouts are washed, then place in a saucepan with a tightly fitting lid and add 1 tsp salt and 1 cup water. Cover and cook over high heat, undisturbed, for 6-7 minutes.

2. Drain well and quickly plunge into a bowl of ice water (this process, known as shocking, stops the cooking process and maintains texture and color). Drain, then toss with the remaining ingredients and serve.

Sigeumchi Namul (Blanched Spinach)

- Prep & Cook Time: 20 min.

Nutrition Info per serving

- Calories 40
- Fat 1.9 g
- Carbohydrates 4.7 g
- Sodium 143 g

Ingredients

- 1 bunch spinach, cleaned, 10-12 ounces
- 2 cloves minced garlic
- 1-2 minced scallions
- ½ tsp sugar
- 1 tsp each: soy sauce, toasted sesame oil, and sesame seeds
- 2 tsps gochujang (optional, for a spicier version)
- Additional tsp soy sauce (optional, for a spicier version)

Preparation

1. Blanch spinach in boiling water, lightly salted, for about 45 seconds, then drain and shock in a bowl of ice water.
2. Let cool, then drain and squeeze out excess water. Chop spinach roughly, then add remaining ingredients. Let meld for about 10 minutes for optimum flavor.

Gaji Namul (Steamed Eggplant)

- Prep & Cook Time: 15 min.

Nutrition Info per serving

- Calories 70
- Fat 2.9 g
- Carbohydrates 10.6 g
- Sodium 456 mg

Ingredients

- 2 medium Asian eggplants cut into 2-inch batons
- 2 minced cloves garlic
- 2 scallions, minced
- 2 tbsps soy sauce
- 2 tsps toasted sesame oil
- ½ tsp sugar
- ½ tsp gochugaru
- 1 tsp sesame seeds

Preparation

1. Steam eggplant until tender but not mushy, about 3-5 minutes.
2. Let cool slightly, toss with remaining ingredients.

Watercress Namul

- Prep & Cook Time: 15 min.

Nutrition Info per serving

- Calories 22
- Fat 1.6g
- Carbohydrates 1.3g
- Sodium 12mg

Ingredients:

- 2 bunches watercress (about 12 ounces)
- 2 minced scallions
- 2 minced cloves garlic
- 1 tsp each toasted sesame oil and sesame seeds
  Salt to taste

Preparation

1. Blanch trimmed and cleaned watercress in boiling, salted water for 45 seconds. Shock in a bowl of ice water and drain when cool.
2. Squeeze excess water out of cress, chop, and toss with remaining ingredients.

Mu Namul (Stir-fried Radish)

- Prep & Cook Time: 15 min.

Nutrition Info per serving

- Calories 90
- Fat 6.3 g
- Carbohydrates 8.2 g
- Sodium 328 mg

Ingredients

- 2 large daikon radish, peeled
- 1 tbsp neutral oil
- 2 minced cloves garlic
- 2 scallions, minced
- 2 tsps toasted sesame oil
- 1 tsp sesame seeds

Preparation

1. Cut the radish into matchsticks.
2. Over medium-high, heat oil, stir fry the radish with ½ tsp salt and garlic for roughly 5 minutes.
3. Add 3 tbsps of water, turn down to medium-low, and cover. Continue cooking until radish is tender, another 3 minutes.
4. Add garlic, scallions, sesame oil and seeds, toss, and serve.

Other Banchan

There are many other categories of banchan, as well, such as hoe (raw or lightly blanched seafood), jorim (simmered dishes), muk (grain porridges), pyeonyuk (boiled and pressed meat), po (dried meat), seon (stuffed dishes), and ssam (wrapped dishes). See below for a variety of other types of banchan to round out your Korean meal.

Kongjang (Dried Beans in Soy)

- Prep & Cook Time: 45 min. plus 6 hours soaking time

Nutrition Info per serving

- Calories 264
- Fat 9.3 g
- Carbohydrates 28.4 g
- Sodium 968 mg

Ingredients

- 1 cup dried soybeans (yellow or black)
- 4 tbsps soy sauce
- 2 tbsps sugar
- 2 tbsps of rice wine
- 1 tbsp corn syrup

Preparation

1. Soak the dried beans for 6 hours. Drain.
2. Put beans with 2 cups water in a pot and let come to a boil for 5 minutes, then skim the surface of any foam.
3. Add soy, sugar, and rice wine and lightly boil for about 30 minutes, uncovered, allowing the beans to absorb the sauce.
4. Add the corn syrup at the very end of cooking, and stir to coat. This can be served immediately or at room temperature, sprinkled with sesame seeds if desired.

Gamja Jorim (Braised Potatoes)

- Prep & Cook Time: 30 min.

Nutrition Info per serving

- Calories 214
- Fat 5.2g
- Carbohydrates 40g
- Sodium 731mg

Ingredients

- 3 medium potatoes, peeled
- ½ green bell pepper
- 1 carrot, peeled
- ½ white onion
- 1 tbsp sugar
- 3 tbsp soy sauce
- 1 tbsp rice wine
- 2 minced cloves garlic
- 1 tbsp honey
- 1 tbsp neutral oil
- 1 tsp each toasted sesame oil and sesame seeds

Preparation

1. Cut the vegetables into 1-inch pieces. Mix soy, sugar, rice wine, garlic, honey and ½ cup of water in a bowl.
2. Heat tbsp oil in a pan and cook potatoes and carrot for about 5 minutes. Add sauce and heat to a boil, then cover and lower heat, cooking until potatoes are tender, roughly 7 minutes.
3. Toss in onion, bell pepper and simmer uncovered for another 5 minutes. Drizzle with sesame oil and seeds and serve.

Dubu Jorim (Braised Tofu)

- Prep & Cook Time: 25 min.

Nutrition Info per serving

- Calories 147
- Fat 11.6 g
- Carbohydrates 4.6 g
- Sodium 461 mg

Ingredients

- 1 pound soft tofu
- 2 tbsp neutral oil
- 2 tbsp soy sauce
- 1 tsp gochugaru
- 1 minced clove garlic
- 2 minced scallions
- 1 tsp sugar
- 1 tsp sesame seeds
- ¼ water

Preparation

1. Cut tofu into ½ inch thick slices. On a skillet, heat oil over medium-high heat and fry tofu, turning once, until slightly browned, about 2 minutes a side.

2. Mix together remaining ingredients and pour over tofu. Cover pan, decrease heat to low and cook for about 10 minutes, so tofu is cooked and coated with sauce. Transfer tofu to plate and drizzle with sauce.

Oi Muchim (Cucumber Salad)

- Prep & Cook Time: 20 min.

Nutrition Info per serving

- Calories 42
- Fat 1.7 g
- Carbohydrates 6.7 g
- Sodium 585 mg

Ingredients

- 2 Kirby cucumbers or 1 English cucumber
- 1 minced clove garlic
- 1 scallion, minced
- 1 tbsp gochugaru
- 1 tsp of rice wine vinegar
- ½ tsp sugar
- 1 tsp each toasted sesame oil and sesame seeds

Preparation

1. Cut cucumbers into rounds (no need to de-seed if using English cucumber). Rub 1 tsp. salt into rounds and let sit for 15 minutes.
2. Drain well and mix in all other ingredients.

Mu Saengchae (Spicy Radish Salad)

- Prep & Cook Time: 30 min.

Nutrition Info per serving

- Calories 29
- Fat .5g
- Carbohydrates 5.8g
- Sodium 833mg

Ingredients

- 1 large daikon radish, peeled
- 3 minced cloves garlic
- 3 scallions, minced
- 2 tbsp gochugaru
- 2 tsps fish sauce
- ½ tsp sugar
- 1 tsp sesame seeds

Preparation

1. Cut daikon into matchsticks and sprinkle with 1 tsp. salt, rubbing in well. Let sit for about 20 minutes, then drain off excess liquid.
2. Mix with remaining ingredients. Check for seasoning, and dash with more fish sauce if necessary.

Putbaechu Doenjang Muchim (Soybean Paste Cabbage)

- Prep & Cook Time: 40 min.

Nutrition Info per serving

- Calories 52
- Fat 3 g
- Carbohydrates 4.8 g
- Sodium 137 mg

Ingredients

- 1 head Napa Cabbage
- 1-2 tbsp doengjang
- 2 tsps toasted sesame oil
- 1 tsp. sesame seeds

Preparation

1. Bring salted water to a boil in a pot. Remove tough core of cabbage, and separate cabbage into leaves. Boil until white part of cabbage is tender, about 5 minutes.
2. Drain and shock in ice water to halt cooking. Squeeze excess liquid out of cabbage leaves.
3. Cut cabbage into 2-inch lengths and toss with remaining ingredients. Let meld for at least 20 minutes before serving.

Goguma Mattang (Candied Sweet Potatoes)

- Prep & Cook Time: 45 min.

Nutrition Info per serving

- Calories 238
- Fat 7.9g
- Carbohydrates 41g
- Sodium 10mg

Ingredients

- 1 pound sweet potatoes
- Neutral cooking oil (for frying) + 1 tbsps
- 3 tbsp sugar
- 2 tsps sesame seeds

Preparation

1. Peel and cut sweet potatoes into ½ inch chunks. Soak in cold water to remove excess starch, about 30 minutes. Draw off water and dry well.
2. Heat enough oil in large skillet to cover potatoes. The oil should register 350 before adding sweet potatoes.
3. Fry sweet potatoes until cooked through, about 7 minutes, then transfer with slotted spoon to paper towels or a brown paper bag to drain off oil.

4. Put the final tbsp of oil in a saute pan and stir in the sugar. Cook over medium-high until sugar melts and starts to caramelize. Turn heat to low and add cooked drained sweet potatoes. Toss well with sauce then garnish with sesame seeds.

Soy Sauce Eggs

- Prep & Cook Time: 30 min.

Nutrition Info per serving

- Calories 130
- Fat 7.5 g
- Carbohydrates 5.7 g
- Sodium 1074 mg

Ingredients

- 6 large eggs, hard boiled
- 2 tbsp of rice wine
- 4 tbsp soy sauce
- 1 shallot or fat green onion

Preparation

1. Peel the eggs. Add all other ingredients to the saucepan along with a cup of water and raise to a boil.
2. Add eggs to saucepan, lower the heat, and simmer for about 15 minutes so the sauce is reduced by half. Roll the eggs around during cooking so that entire egg gets coated in sauce.
3. Cool eggs, slice and serve at room temperature or cold.

GimGui (Toasted Seaweed)

- Prep & Cook Time: 5 min.

Nutrition Info per serving

- Calories 43
- Fat 4g
- Carbohydrates 0g
- Sodium5mg

Ingredients

- 8 sheets of dried seaweed (often found under their Japanese name, nori)
- 1 tsp toasted sesame oil
- 1 tbsp neutral oil
- Salt

Preparation

1. Arrange sheets shiny side up. Mix oils in a small bowl and brush shiny side with oil. Salt lightly.
2. Place under the broiler for 5-10 seconds, being careful not to let sheets burn. Alternatively, suspend over a gas flame, rotating to cook evenly
3. Let cool, then cut into squares. Makes for a nice snack, as well.

Ssamjang (Dipping Sauce)

While not actually a banchan side dish, ssamjang is a frequent accompaniment to Korean meals, as the most renowned dipping sauce for a wide variety of foods, particularly grilled meats (see Chapter 4). It can be bought pre-made but is also easy to make at home if you've stocked your Korean pantry well.

Mix together

- ¼ cup doenjang with 1-2 tbsp of gochujang, according to your preferred spice level.
- Add minced garlic clove and a couple of minced scallions, 2 tsps each of honey and toasted sesame oil, and 1 tsp sesame seeds.

Kimchi and Other Pickles

The significance of kimchi to Korean cuisine cannot be overstated. Some form of kimchi is served with nearly every meal of every type. It would not be an overstatement to suggest that kimchi is the national dish of Korea. While you can purchase kimchi in Asian markets and some grocery stores, it is fairly simple and very satisfying to make at home. All it takes is patience! What follows here are some traditional recipes for making kimchi, adjusted for the home cook, as well as some shortcuts for quicker pickles to make and eat that day.

Kimchi

Traditional Cabbage Kimchi

- Prep Time: 1 hr.
- Total Time: 12 hrs. plus fermentation time 3-6 days
- Yields: about 1 ½ quart

Ingredients

- 2 pounds Napa cabbage, cut into roughly 2-inch pieces
- 6 scallions, chopped finely or slivered
- 6 minced cloves of garlic
- 1 ½ tbsp fresh ginger, peeled and minced
- 2 tbsps gochugaru (or other red chili powder but with caution)
- 1 or 2 tsps of sugar

Preparation

1. Make brine with 3 tbsp of salt and 6 cups of water.
2. Place chopped cabbage in a large bowl or nonreactive pot (or, if you've been industrious with shopping, a Korean onggi) and ladle brine over cabbage. Weigh down with something (plate, platter) to keep the cabbage submerged and let this sit out for 12 hours.
3. Now remove cabbage, but reserve the brine. Toss cabbage with a tsp of salt and all else remaining. Pack this mixture into a 2-quart jar (or, alternatively, 2 1 quart jars: old,

washed mayonnaise jars work) and pour brine over just to cover.

4. Take a freezer or sandwich storage bag and push it into the mouth of the jar. Pour remaining brine into the bag and seal it; this keeps the cabbage submerged in the brine while allowing the bubbles caused by fermentation to escape. (If the jar is sealed, it could shatter from the pressure released during fermentation.)

5. Allow the kimchi to ferment in a cool place, ideally around 68 degrees (a garage in cool weather works, or an inner closet during warmer weather), for about 3-6 days. It will get sourer as time passes.

6. Remove the bag with brine and seal your jar tightly. Your kimchi should keep in the refrigerator for months.

Quick Kimchi

- Prep Time: 20-25 min. Brining time: 48 hours.
- Yields: 1 ½ quart

Ingredients

- Napa cabbage, head, sliced into 1-inch squares
- 2 tbsp sugar
- 2 tbsp kosher or sea salt
- 10 cloves of garlic, minced
- 10 scallions, minced
- 2 tbsp of grated ginger
- ¼-1/2 cup gochugaru (more chili powder yields hotter kimchi)
- ¼ soy sauce
- ¼ fish sauce (optional but it does mimic the fermented flavor of the more traditional recipe)

Preparation

1. Toss the cabbage with the sugar and salt in a nonreactive container; rub seasonings in well. Refrigerate overnight.
2. The next day mix together the remaining ingredients, adding water if the brine is too thick; it should have the consistency of a creamy-style salad dressing. Drain the cabbage and add it to your briny mixture.
3. Pack into the jar(s) and refrigerate. It will be good in another 24 hours but even better as it absorbs flavors over time.

Kkaekdugi (Radish Kimchi)

Follow the previous recipe, substituting three medium daikon radishes (large white radishes, available in most grocery stores). Be sure to peel them and cut into ½ inch chunks. Radish kimchi is excellent in hearty stews, bringing a satisfying sour crunch to balance the richness of the stew.

Baek-kimchi (Chili free Kimchi or "White Kimchi")

This kimchi is good for those with a low tolerance for heat (such as younger children). It is a light somewhat sweet pickle with just a touch of fermented flavor. If you want to up the funky flavor, add 2-4 tbsp of fish sauce to the brine.

- Prep Time: about 2hrs, largely unattended.
- Brining time: 3 days
- Yields: 1 ½ quart

Ingredients
- 1 Napa cabbage, quartered
- ¼ cup kosher or coarse sea salt dissolved in 4 cups water

Puree:

- 1 tbsp kosher or coarse sea salt
- 1 Asian or Bosc pear, peeled and cored
- 1 small red apple, peeled and cored
- 1 large or 2 small shallots
- 3 minced cloves garlic
- 1 tsp grated ginger
- 4 cups of water

Preparation

1. Soak the cabbage quarters in the brine, weighed down with a plate, for about 1 ½ hour. Drain well.
2. Meanwhile, puree the additional water and salt, pear, apple, shallot, garlic, and ginger in a food processor or blender. Push this mixture through a fine sieve to remove coarse food particles, toss with cabbage quarters. Cover loosely, then leave at cool room temperature for 12-24 hours to ferment.
3. Transfer to the refrigerator for another 3-7 days (it gets sourer as you leave it). This kimchi does not keep as long as others, about two weeks.

Dongkimchi (Winter Kimchi)

- Prep Time: 1 hr.
- Brining time: 2 hrs. plus 2 days to 2 weeks
- Yields: 1 ½ quart

Ingredients

- ½ Napa cabbage, chopped into 2-inch pieces
- 2 daikon radishes, chopped into 1-inch pieces
- 3 tbsp coarse salt
- 1 tbsps sugar
- 1 small Asian pear, peeled and cored
- 1-inch piece of ginger
- 5 cloves of garlic
- 1 shallot
- 2-3 red or green chilis, slivered
- 2 scallions, slivered

Preparation

1. Make a brine for the cabbage with 2 tbsp salt and 1 cup of water. Combine and let stand, weighted down with a plate, for a couple of hours.
2. Toss the radish pieces with a tbsp of salt and the sugar and set aside for 30 minutes.
3. Drain both cabbage and radish well, rinsing off excess salt

if you like, though it should remain a bit salty. Reserve the brine from cabbage and any liquid exuded by radishes.

4. Puree pear, garlic, ginger and shallot with ½ cup of water; strain this, if desired, then add to reserved brine.

5. Toss cabbage and radish with chilis and scallions, pack into the jar(s) and pour seasoned brine over. If you need more brine to cover, mix 2 tbsp of salt with an additional 4 cups of water, and use this to cover.

6. Leave dongkimchi out at cool room temp for two days then put in refrigerator for another 2 weeks. It is ready to eat any time after the initial 2 days but gets more complex with time. This keeps for a couple of months.

Nabak-kimchi (Spring Kimchi)

Spring kimchi is very similar to winter kimchi, with the addition of some carrot for a different flavor and more color (1-2 small carrots, slivered). Both winter and spring kimchis are often prepared with slurry made from rice flour and water; this gives the "water kimchi" a bit of body and a touch of sweetness. If you like, mix 1 tbsp of sweet rice flour with a cup of water and add this along with the brine mixture in Step 5 in the previous recipe.

Oisobagi (Cucumber Kimchi)

- Prep Time: 30-40 min.
- Brining: 15 min. to 2 weeks
- Yields: 1 quart

Ingredients

- 1 pound Kirby cucumbers (small unwaxed cucumbers), cut into ½ inch spears
- 1 ½ tsps salt
- 2 ½ tbsp sugar
- 1 ½ tbsp gochugaru
- 1 tbsp of grated ginger
- 3 cloves of garlic, thinly sliced
- 1 tbsp each soy sauce and fish sauce
- 2 scallions, slivered
- 1 shallot, thinly sliced

Preparation

1. Toss cucumber spears with ½ tsp of the salt and ½ tbsp of the sugar. Leave them to macerate for about ten minutes.
2. Combine the remaining ingredients in a bowl, dissolving salt and sugar thoroughly and add drained cucumbers. Let this sit for at least 15 minutes before serving, but they will keep in the refrigerator for up to 2 weeks.

Pakimchi (Scallion Kimchi)

- Prep Time: 20 min. Brining Time: 1 day to 2 weeks
- Yields: 1 quart

Ingredients

- 1 pound scallions
- 4 tbsp gochugaru
- 4 tbsp fish sauce
- 2 tsps sugar
- 1 tsp grated ginger
- 2-3 minced cloves garlic

Preparation

1. Mix together all ingredients except scallions into a nice paste, then rub into cleaned and trimmed scallions (left whole).
2. Pack into a jar or place into a Ziploc bag and squeeze the air out. Leave to ferment at cool room temperature for 1 day, then refrigerate. It can be eaten immediately or stored for up to 3 weeks.

Kkaennip Kimchi (Perilla Leaf Kimchi)

Perilla leaf is related to Japanese shiso and a member of the mint family. It is used often in Korean and is worth seeking out at Asian markets during the summer months.

- Prep Time: 20 min.
- Brining Time: 3 hours to 3 weeks
- Yields: 1 ½ cups

Ingredients

- 50 Perilla leaves
- 2 tbsps gochugaru
- 1 tbsp each fish sauce and soy sauce
- 1 minced clove garlic
- 1 tsp sesame seeds, preferably toasted
- ½ cup water or vegetable broth or dashi (light seaweed broth)

Preparation

1. Be sure that perilla leaves are rinsed and dried well. Mix together remaining ingredients, then rub the paste into each individual leaf, stacking as you go.
3. When all leaves are coated, transfer to storage container, pour over any remaining spice mixture and seal. Leave out for 3 hours, then refrigerate and use within 3 weeks.

Jangajii

Jangajii is the general name for pickles in Korean. Unlike kimchis, these are not fermented. There are three basic methods for pickling in Korean cuisine, as explored below.

Soy Sauce Pickles

- Prep Time: 20 min. Total Time: 3 days
- Yield: 1 quart

Ingredients

- 1 pound Kirby cucumbers (small unwaxed cucumbers)
- 3 cups soy sauce
- 3 cups of sugar
- 3 cups of rice wine vinegar
- Garlic, chilis, scallions optional

Preparation

1. Bring soy sauce, sugar, and vinegar to a boil, then switch off heat and let it stand. Next, prepare the cucumbers.
2. Rub cucumbers with enough coarse salt to coat, massaging salt into the cucumber to scrub the peel and begin to make it malleable. Rinse, then pack into the jar(s) and cover with soy sauce mixture (you can leave cucumbers whole—

these stay crisper for longer—or cut into thick rounds). Add any optional ingredients, roughly chopped, for flavor, if you like.
3. Let cucumbers sit out for 3 days, then refrigerate. These will last for a couple of months, growing stronger by the day.

This method works for all sorts of vegetables in roughly the same ratios, keeping soy to sugar to rice wine vinegar 1:1:1. Try a mix of whole garlic cloves and scallions; fresh green beans during the summer; or small boiling onions: experiment and enjoy!

Doenjang (Soybean) Pickles

- Prep Time: 15 min.
- Total Time: 1 week to 2 months
- Yield: 1 quart

Ingredients

- 1 lb. cucumbers, preferably English
- 1 cup doenjang (fermented soybean paste)
- ¼ cup of rice wine
- 1 tbsp sugar
- 1 tsp soy sauce

Preparation

1. Mix all ingredients together except for cucumbers. Scrub cucumbers well, then pack into the jar(s) and cover with doenjang mixture.
2. Refrigerate for at least 1 week before using and up to 2 months.

Like soy sauce pickles, this basic formula can be used for a wide variety of vegetables (green beans, radish, eggplant) and as a marinade for fish and meats (marinate skinless fish or chicken, cubed pork or beef overnight in the pickling mixture, then grill).

Brined Pickles

Truly, nothing could be simpler than traditional methods of Korean brined pickles. Simply use a ratio of water to salt at 10:1 (so, 10 cups of water needs 1 cup of salt). Bring brine to boil for about 5 minutes, cool slightly, pour over 2 pounds of vegetables while still hot. This won't cook the vegetables but will allow the brine to penetrate the flesh while maintaining crispness. Let stand at cool room temperature, weighted down, for 2 to 3 days, then pack into the jar(s), seal, and refrigerate for up to 1 month.

If a whitish film forms on the surface of brine, simply pour brine off, boil again for about 5 minutes before returning to the jar(s) and refrigerating.

Cucumbers are still the standard vegetable here but experiment with whatever is fresh and in season. Parboil sturdy vegetables like carrots when using this method.

Jjeotgal

Jjeotgal is the Korean term for "salted seafood." It can refer to a wide variety of condiments and side dishes, from its liquefied form (aekjeot: fish sauce) to pasty or chunky condiments that are served as part of the banchan (small dishes) of the Korean meal. The variety in Korean markets can be virtually endless in terms of the seafood used. Most forms of jjeotgal are purchased rather than made at home, but it can be done.

Essentially, clean and generously salt your choice of seafood, leaving it to cure for about six hours. Meanwhile, bring soy sauce, garlic, scallions, gochujang, ginger, and a bit of sugar to a boil (ratios depend on the amount of seafood, but about 2 cups of soy sauce to 1 pound of seafood with other ingredients included to taste). Pour while hot over salted seafood, then let stand for another hour. Drain and repeat this process another 5 or 6 times.

Soups & Stews

As detailed in Chapter 1, the geography and climate of Korea call for hearty, warming food. And what could better fit that need than delicious, often spicy soups and stews?

There are different categories of Korean soups and stews: **guk** and **tang** are thinner varieties, more like soup, while **jeongol** and **jjigae** are thicker, more like stews.

See below for recipes that will keep you cozy all winter long—and throughout the year!

Note on the stock: homemade stocks are always better than canned.

Korean cooking often uses a dried anchovy stock which is very simple to make:

1. *boil a dozen plump dried anchovies in 6 cups of water for 10 minutes, then strain.*

2. *Substitutions, such as chicken or vegetable stock, while less authentic, can be utilized.*

Kimchi KongnamulGuk (Kimchi & Bean Sprout Soup)

- Prep & Cooking Time: 30 minutes
- For 4 servings

Nutrition Info per serving

- Fat 1.1 g
- Carbohydrates 6.2 g
- Sodium 1721 mg
- Calories 49

Ingredients

- 6 cups of stock
- 1 package bean sprouts (about 12 ounces)
- ½ cup cabbage kimchi
- ¼ cup liquid from kimchi

- 2 tsps fish sauce
- 2 minced cloves garlic
- 2 scallions, minced
- 1-2 tsps gochugaru (optional, for spicier results)

Preparation

1. Bring stock to a simmer. Rinse sprouts and chop kimchi into ½ inch pieces.
2. Add kimchi, kimchi liquid, and fish sauce to stock and lightly boil for 7-8 minutes until kimchi is almost tender.
3. Add bean sprouts and garlic and simmer for another 3 minutes. Toss in scallions and gochugaru, if using, and let flavors meld for a couple of minutes. Serve over rice.

Baechu Doengjang Guk (Cabbage Soup with Soybean Paste)

- Prep & Cooking Time: 30 min.
- For 4 servings

Nutrition Info per serving

- Calories 64
- Fat 1 g
- Carbohydrates 11.2 g
- Sodium 1387 mg

Ingredients

- 4 cups stock (beef is also good here)
- 2 tbsp doenjang
- 1 tbsp soy sauce
- 1-2 tsps gochujang
- 1 head Napa cabbage
- 2 cloves garlic, minced
- 2 scallions, minced

Preparation

1. Start to simmer stock. Add doenjang, soy sauce, and gochujang to stock and whisk to make sure the ingredients are fully incorporated.

2. Cut cabbage into 2-inch pieces and add to stock. Simmer for about 15 minutes, until cabbage is done.
3. Toss in garlic and scallions and simmer for another 5-7 minutes.

Ganjaguk (Potato Soup)

- Prep & Cook Time: 40 min.
- Yield: 4 servings

Nutrition Info per serving

- Calories 233
- Fat 4.4 g
- Carbohydrates 32.8 g
- Sodium 154 mg

Ingredients

- 3 ounces of rice noodles
- 1/4 pound beef stew meat
- ½ tbsp soy sauce
- 2 cloves garlic, minced
- 3 medium potatoes
- ½ pound tofu
- 3 scallions

Preparation

1. For 20 minutes, soak rice noodles in lukewarm water, while preparing other ingredients.
2. Toss meat with soy sauce and garlic and let marinate while prepping remaining ingredients.

3. Peel and cut potatoes into ½ inch half moons. Cut tofu into slices of equal size. Cut scallions into 1-inch lengths.
4. Saute beef until browned, about 5 minutes, then put in 6 cups of water. Heat to a boil, then cover and simmer for 5 minutes.
5. Add potatoes and tofu, along with salt to taste, and cook potatoes until soft, about 5 minutes.
6. Add drained rice noodles and scallions and simmer for another 2 minutes. Serve hot.

Tteokguk (Rice Cake Soup)

- Prep & Cooking Time: 2 hours, mostly unattended
- For 4 servings

Nutrition Info per serving

- Calories 471
- Fat 5.3 g
- Carbohydrates 77g
- Sodium266 mg

Ingredients

- ½ pound beef, preferably brisket
- ½ white or yellow onion
- 6 cloves of garlic
- 3 scallions
- 1 tbsp (or more) soy sauce
- 1 tsp toasted sesame oil
- 4 cups sliced rice cake
- Sliced scallions and toasted nori (seaweed) for garnish

Preparation

1. Bring brisket, onion, garlic, scallions and 13 cups of lightly salted water to a boil in a large pot. Clear the surface of any foam that rises. Lower heat, cover, and simmer beef until tender, about 1 ½ hour.

2. Drain, reserving broth, and discard vegetables. Season broth with a tbsp of soy sauce. Shred beef into bite-size pieces and toss with a little bit of soy sauce and sesame oil. Reserve.
3. While beef is cooking or cooling, soak rice cakes in water to cover for about 20 minutes. Return seasoned broth to a boil and drop in drained rice cakes. Simmer for about 7 minutes.
4. Ladle broth and rice cakes into bowls and divide beef equally among each serving. Garnish with scallions and nori. This dish is often made at Korean New Year's celebrations.

Oi Naengguk (Cold Cucumber Soup)

- Prep & Cooking Time: 10 minutes
- For 4 servings

Nutrition Info per serving

- Calories 84
- Fat 1.4 g
- Carbohydrates 17.4 g
- Sodium 89 mg

Ingredients

- 3 Kirby cucumbers or 1 English cucumber
- 1 minced clove garlic
- 1 minced scallion
- 1 minced fresh red chili or 1 tsp gochugaru (optional, for a spicier version)
- 1 ½ tsps salt
- 1 tsp each sugar and soy sauce
- 2 tsps rice wine vinegar
- 1 cup water with 1 cup ice cubes
- 6 cherry tomatoes, quartered (optional)
- 2 tsps sesame seeds

Preparation

1. Cut cucumber into matchsticks and toss with garlic, scallion, chili (if using), salt, sugar, soy, and vinegar. Make sure salt and sugar are thoroughly dissolved. Let flavors meld for a couple of minutes.
2. Add water, ice cubes, and tomatoes (if using) and garnish with sesame seeds. Serve right away.

Dak Gomtang (Chicken Soup)

This is a very basic template for a bowl of Korean inflected chicken soup. It can certainly be customized with any number of additions: some gochujang for spice, or doenjang for funk; soaked rice noodles or cooked rice for heartiness; or cooked vegetables for freshness.

- Prep & Cooking Time: 2 hours, mostly unattended
- Yield: 6-8 servings

Nutrition Info per serving

- Calories 415
- Fat 15.6 g
- Carbohydrates 3.7 g
- Sodium 184 mg

Ingredients

- 1 whole chicken, 3-4 pounds
- 1 yellow onion
- 3 scallions
- 1-inch piece of ginger
- 1 tsp black peppercorns
- Chopped kimchi and sliced scallions, for garnish

Preparation

1. Put all ingredients in large pot, add 10-12 cups of water (enough to cover chicken), and bring to a boil. Clear the surface of any foam that rises.
2. Decrease heat and simmer, covered, for 45 minutes, until chicken is cooked through and tender. Drain, reserving broth and chicken. Discard vegetables.
3. Wait until chicken has cooled, then shred meat into small pieces, disposing of skin and bones.
4. Skim fat off broth if desired, then return chicken to broth (add any additional seasoning at this time, if you like). Serve over rice or noodles and top with kimchi and scallions.

Yukgaejang (Spicy Beef and Vegetable Soup)

- Prep & Cooking Time:2 hours, mostly unattended
- For4 servings

Nutrition Info per serving

- Calories 328
- Fat 14.4 g
- Carbohydrates 11.3 g
- Sodium 242 mg

Ingredients

- 1 pound beef brisket
- ½ white onion
- ½ pound daikon radish
- 3 whole cloves garlic

- ½ cup dried fernbrake (gosari, available at Asian markets)
- 3 dried or 6 fresh shitake mushrooms
- 1 cup bean sprouts
- 2 bundles scallions, coarsely chopped
- 2 tbsp toasted sesame oil
- 2 tbsp minced garlic
- 2 tbsp gochujang
- 2 tsps gochugaru
- 2 tsps soy sauce

Preparation

1. Put beef, onion, radish, and garlic cloves in the large pot. Cover with 14 cups of water and heat to a boil. Clear surface of any foam that rises. Lower to a simmer, top with lid, and cook until meat is falling apart about 1 ½ hours.
2. While meat is cooking, soak gosari and, if using, dried mushrooms for at least 30 minutes.
3. Drain meat, reserving broth, and when cool enough to handle, shred.
4. Toss shredded meat with soaked gosari, sliced mushrooms (fresh or soaked dried), bean sprouts, and scallions. Mix in minced garlic, sesame oil, gochujang, gochugaru, and soy. Return to broth and simmer for 10 minutes for flavors to meld. Adjust seasoning and serve hot.

Galbitang (Beef Short Rib Soup)

- Prep & Cook Time: 2 hours, some unattended
- Yield: 4 servings

Nutrition Info per serving

- Calories 1033
- Fat 82g
- Carbohydrates 28.7g
- Sodium566mg

Ingredients

- 3 pounds flanken cut (across the bone) short ribs
- 1 large daikon radish
- 1 white onion
- 3 whole scallions
- 5 cloves of garlic
- 3 thick slices of ginger
- 2 tbsp soy sauce
- 3 ounces sweet potato noodles
- 2 cloves garlic, minced
- 2 scallions, sliced
- Soy sauce, some pepper, and salt if you like

Preparation

1. Parboil the ribs: drop in a pot of boiling water for about 10 minutes, then drain and rinse. This step can be skipped but it removes impurities that might leach from the bones in the meat.
2. Cover ribs with 14 cups of water and add radish, onion, scallions, garlic, ginger, and soy. Simmer until meat is done about 1 ½ hours.
3. Remove radish from broth about 30 minutes into cooking, then chop into bite-sized pieces when cool enough to handle. Discard other vegetables.
4. Cover sweet potato noodles with water and soak for 30 minutes, then add to soup along with reserved radish and minced garlic. Cook for another 5 minutes or so for flavors to meld, and adjust seasonings. Served garnished with sliced scallions.

Haemul Jeongol (Seafood Hot Pot)

- Prep & Cooking Time:45 minutes
- For 4 servings

Nutrition Info per serving

- Calories 224
- Fat 3.7 g
- Carbohydrates 18 g
- Sodium 637 mg

Ingredients

- ¾ pound shrimp, deveined
- ¾ pound mussels, cleaned
- ½ cup sliced daikon radish
- 4 thinly sliced shiitake mushrooms, thinly sliced
- 1 small thinly sliced zucchini
- ½ cup bean sprouts
- 5 cups of water
- 1-ounce kombu (dried kelp)

For Sauce

- 2-3 Tbsp gochugaru
- 3 cloves garlic, minced
- 1 tbsp soy sauce
- 2 tbsp of rice wine
- ½ tbsp fish sauce

Preparation

1. Peel shrimp and reserve shells. Bring 5 cups water, cleaned mussels, and shrimp shells to a bowl in a large saucepan. Cover and cook until mussels just open, about 5-7 minutes. Strain, reserving broth and mussels. Discard shells.
2. Bring reserved broth back to boil and add kombu. Simmer for another 10 minutes, then remove and discard kombu.
3. Mix together sauce ingredients, ensure it is at the spice level you wish. Stir this into the broth and add radish. Cook for about 5 minutes, until radish, is tender.
4. Put everything left into the pot, bring the broth back to a hard simmer and serve as soon as seafood is cooked through about 5 minutes.

Bulgogi Jeongol (Beef Hot Pot)

- Prep & Cooking Time: 30 minutes plus overnight marinating
- For 4 servings

Nutrition Info per serving

- Calories 508
- Fat 12.9 g
- Carbohydrates 55 g
- Sodium 1522 mg

Ingredients

For marinade:

- 6 tbsp soy sauce
- 2 tbsp of rice wine
- 3 tbsp sugar
- 5 minced cloves garlic
- 1 Asian pear, peeled
- ½ white onion
- 1 tsp grated ginger
- Black pepper

For Hot Pot:

- ¾ pound beef, such as sirloin
- 4 ½ cups anchovy stock
- 5 ounces tofu, cut into small to medium squares

- ½ pound shitake mushrooms stemmed and thinly sliced
- 3 ounces sweet potato noodles, soaked in water for 20 minutes
- ¼ pound Napa cabbage, chopped into ½ inch pieces
- 2 scallions, sliced
- 1 red chili, sliced (optional)

Preparation

1. Blend all marinade ingredients in processor or blender. Slice beef paper thin (this is easier to do if you first freeze the meat for about 30 minutes, then slice) and toss with 1 cup of marinade. Marinate beef for at least 4 hours and up to overnight for best flavor. Reserve remaining marinade.
2. When ready to serve, mix stock with reserved marinade. Place beef in center of the large pot, arranging the rest of the prepared ingredients in small piles around it. Pour broth mixture over this and heat to a boil. Let bubble for about 10 minutes, serve over cooked rice.

Kimchi Jjigae (Kimchi Stew)

- Prep & Cook Time: 1 hour
- Yield: 4 servings

Nutrition Info per serving

- Calories 215
- Fat 14g
- Carbohydrates 5g
- Sodium 1002mg

Ingredients

- ¼ pound bacon
- 1 small onion, chopped
- 2 cups cabbage kimchi, chopped
- ½ cup kimchi liquid
- 2 tbsp gochugaru
- 1 tbsp gochujang
- ½ pound firm tofu, sliced
- 2 scallions, thinly sliced, for garnish

Preparation

1. Cut bacon into ¼ strips and cook over medium heat in a pot until browned, roughly 3 minutes. Pour off most of the fat, then add onion and soften it, roughly 5 minutes. Add chopped kimchi and liquid, turn heat to medium-high,

and sizzle until kimchi softens and liquid evaporates, about 5 minutes.
2. Add gochugaru and gochujang, along with 2 cups of water. Cook at a simmer for 30 minutes.
3. Put tofu in the pan and cook for another 3-5 minutes, and serve stew garnished with scallions.

Haemul Sundubu Jjigae (Seafood and Tofu Stew)

- Prep & Cooking Time: 30 minutes
- For 4 servings

Nutrition Info per serving

- Calories 197
- Fat 7.9 g
- Carbohydrates 9.4 g
- Sodium 1061 mg

Ingredients

- 1 tbsp neutral oil
- ½ white onion, finely chopped
- 2 sliced scallions
- 2 minced cloves garlic
- ½ cup chopped cabbage kimchi
- ¼ cup kimchi liquid
- 3 tbsp gochugaru
- 3 tbsp soy sauce
- 14 ounces silken tofu
- 8 large shrimp, peeled
- ¼ pound squid, cut into rings
- 12 mussels, cleaned
- 1 large egg yolk (optional: egg will not be fully cooked)

Preparation

1. Heat oil over medium; add onion, scallion, and garlic. Soften everything for about 10 minutes. Add kimchi and liquid and saute for a little bit longer, about a minute.
2. Add gochugaru, soy, and 2 cups water. Heat to a simmer and cook until flavors come together, 5-6 minutes.
3. Put tofu in center of the pot, trying not to break it up, and encircle it with the seafood. Put the lid on and cook until mussels open, around 5 minutes.
4. Remove stew from burner and top with egg yolk, if using. Divide among bowls, breaking up yolk and tofu as you go.

Hobak Gochujang Jjigae (Spicy Zucchini Stew)

- Prep & Cooking Time: 30 minutes
- For 4 servings

Nutrition Info per serving

- Calories 154
- Fat 1.1g
- Carbohydrates 27.4 g
- Sodium 605 mg

Ingredients

- 2 medium zucchini
- 2 medium potatoes, peeled
- 2 tbsp gochujang
- 1 tbsp each of doenjang and soy sauce
- 3 green chilis, sliced
- 2 cloves garlic, minced
- 3 ounces ground pork or canned clams (optional: omit for vegetarian version)
- 2 scallions, sliced

Preparation

1. Cut zucchini into ½ inch pieces and potatoes into ¼ inch pieces.

2. Put 4 cups of water in a pot and stir in gochujang, doenjang, and soy. Heat to a boil and be sure ingredients are dissolved.
3. Add zucchini, potatoes and remaining ingredients except for scallions and simmer for 10 minutes, until potatoes yield.
4. Garnish with scallions and serve.

Budae Jjigae (Army Stew)

This is a peculiar stew, borne of a particular time in Korean history: the Korean War and its aftermath. The war brought American army bases and the processed foods needed to sustain soldiers with it; after the war, food was scarce in Korea and, thus, these American staples became a common way to make filling food. Be forewarned: while tasty, this stew packs a sodium punch!

- Prep & Cooking Time: 30 minutes
- For 4-6 servings

Nutrition Info per serving

- Calories 509
- Fat 11.4 g
- Carbohydrates 51.4 g
- Sodium 2343 mg

Ingredients

For sauce:

- 2 tbsp gochugaru
- 1/2 tbsp gochujang
- 3 cloves garlic, minced
- 1/2 tbsps sugar
- 2 tbsp of rice wine
- 1 Tbsp soy sauce

For stew:

- 4 cups stock (preferably chicken)
- 1 can SPAM, sliced
- 2 hot dogs, sliced on the diagonal
- ½ pound firm tofu, sliced ½ inch thick
- 1 pound shitake mushrooms, stems discarded and caps sliced
- ½ cup cabbage kimchi, chopped
- 1 package instant ramen noodles (discard flavoring packet if it comes with one)
- 2 ounces of rice cakes, sliced
- 2 scallions, sliced
- 2 slices American cheese

Preparation

1. Stir together all sauce ingredients.
2. Arrange SPAM, hot dogs, tofu, mushrooms, and kimchi in the pot. Place sauce in the middle. Pour broth over, cover pot, and heat to a boil. Then, lower to a simmer and cook for 5-7 minutes.
3. Add noodles, rice cakes, scallions, and cheese. Cover pot and simmer for another 3 minutes. Divide among bowls, serving over rice.

Saewoojuk (Shrimp and Rice Porridge)

- Prep & Cook Time:1 hr. plus 2 hrs.-overnight soaking
- Yield: 4 servings

Nutrition Info per serving

- Calories 284
- Fat 4.7 g
- Carbohydrates 41.8 g
- Sodium 491 mg

Ingredients

- 1 cup short-grained rice
- 1 tbsp neutral oil
- 2 minced cloves garlic
- ¼ cup carrot, diced
- ½ pound shrimp, peeled and chopped
- 1 tbsp fish sauce
- Sliced scallions and nori (seaweed), for garnish

Preparation

1. Wash rice in a few changes of water, swishing rice around until it looks clear. Drain a final time and add 4 cups of water to rice. Leave to soak for a minimum of 2 hours and up to overnight.

2. Heat oil over medium heat in a pot, saute garlic, carrot, and shrimp for a couple of minutes, coating with oil. Add soaked, drained rice and 7 cups of water to pot and heat to a boil. Cover, lower to a simmer, and let bubble away for 30 minutes.
3. Add fish sauce and salt to taste, then scoop into bowls, garnishing with scallions and nori.

Desserts: Hangwa and Tteok

Hangwa

Hangwa refers to traditional Korean confections in general. The following recipes are a sample of the different categories and a vast variety of Korean sweet finishes that are available to the serious home cook.

Dasik (Tea Cookies)

These cookies are simple, no-bake cookies, typically pressed into a mold especially for them. They are traditionally served at Lunar New Year festivities and are supposed to promote good health.

Green Tea Cookies

- Prep & Cook Time: 10 min.
- Yield: 1 serving

Nutrition Info per serving

- Calories 173
- Fat .4 g
- Carbohydrates 40 g
- Sodium 156 mg

Ingredients

- 3 tbsp rice flour
- 2 tsps powdered sugar
- Pinch of salt
- 1 tsp green tea powder (often called Matcha)
- 2 tsps light honey

Preparation

Mix all ingredients together, along with enough water to make a pliable dough. Press into dasik mold or roll into a thick sheet and cut with decorative cookie cutters. Multiply ingredients according to how many you wish to make of each kind.

Variation: Berry Tea Cookies

Use the same ingredients as above, substituting 2 ½ tsps prepared Omjia (Five Berry) tea in place of green tea powder and water.

Gwapyeon (Fruit Jelly)

These sweets are similar to American jello, with different and fresher fruit flavors and a typically firmer texture, though this is up to the cook. The method below is merely a suggestion: you can add more or less sugar and starch as you desire, as well as modifying the type of fruit and/or starch that you use.

- Prep & Cook Time: 20-30 min. plus 4 hours cooling
- Yield: 4 servings

Nutrition Info per serving

- Calories 190
- Fat 0g
- Carbohydrates 48 g
- Sodium 7 mg

Ingredients

- 1 cup fruit juice/puree, peeled and sieved if necessary (for example, Asian pear, persimmon, tangerine, grape, apple)
- ½ cup of sugar
- ½ cup starch (corn starch, potato starch, rice starch) mixed with 1 ounce water

Preparation

1. Prepare the fruit juice as necessary for the type of fruit and force through a sieve for a smoother texture. Mix well with sugar, sieve again to remove any potential lumps.

2. Stir starch into fruit and sugar mixture and heat to a soft boil. Boil for about 5 minutes, until mixture starts to thicken. Time will vary based on the kind of fruit and starch used.
3. Pour into a container or molds and let cool for 4 hours before cutting into pieces or turning out of molds.

Jeonggwa (Fruit Jerky)

This can be made with various fruits and vegetables, as well. Lotus root is popular. The following recipe uses beets, which are readily available.

- Prep & Cook Time: 1 ½ hour
- Yield: 18 pieces

Nutrition Info per serving

- Calories 200
- Fat 6 g
- Carbohydrates 37g
- Sodium 11 mg

Ingredients

- ½ cup peeled and grated beet
- 1 cup + 2 tbsp sugar
- 2 tbsp lemon juice (be sure to use fresh)
- ½ cup sesame seeds, preferably toasted

Preparation

1. Stir everything together, except seeds, in a heavy pot. Add a touch of salt and gently simmer over low heat, covered, for 40 minutes, stirring occasionally.

2. Remove lid and cook another 20 minutes, stirring frequently. It is done when the jelly drops from the spoon in lumps.
3. Meanwhile, place a sheet of parchment paper on countertop or cutting board and spread with half the sesame seeds. Carefully ladle the beet jelly on top of sesame seeds and sprinkle with another half of seeds.
4. Let cool for about 20 minutes, until still warm but cool enough to handle, and using parchment paper, shape into a log, about 8 inches by 1 ½ inch. Cut the jelly into pieces and serve immediately or wrap in cellophane to store.

Yaksik (Sweet Rice with Nuts and Fruit)

- Prep & Cooking Time: 45 minutes
- For 10 servings

Nutrition Info per serving

- Calories 201
- Fat 5.5g
- Carbohydrates 36 g
- Sodium 182 mg

Ingredients

- ¼ cup of sugar
- ¼ cup dark brown sugar
- 2 tbsps soy sauce
- 1 tbsp toasted sesame oil
- 2 tbsp neutral oil
- ½ tsp cinnamon
- 1 cup dried cranberries
- ¼ raisins
- ¼ cup honey
- 2 tbsp pine nuts
- 1 can water chestnuts, drained
- 4 cups cooked sticky rice

Preparation

1. Mix ¼ cup white sugar with ¼ cup water in a little pan and, over medium heat, cook until sugar caramelizes and becomes a dark brown color, about 8 minutes.
2. Mix together brown sugar, soy, both oils, and cinnamon in a large bowl, then add cooked rice and caramel. Stir together thoroughly.
3. Pack mixture into a steamer lined with cheesecloth and steam for 30 minutes.
4. Turn out into the pan to cool, where you can cut candy into squares or roll into balls.

Yugwa (Sweet Rice Crackers)

Traditionally, these are made from soaked glutinous rice flour in a days-long process. What follows is a handy simplification for the home cook.

- Prep & Cook Time: 35-40 min.
- Yield: 8 servings

Nutrition Info per serving

- Calories 394
- Fat .4 g
- Carbohydrates 95 g
- Sodium 3 mg

Ingredients

- 2 cups of sugar
- 3 thick slices ginger
- Neutral oil, for frying
- 1 pound tube-shaped rice cakes
- Sesame seeds

Preparation

1. Make sugar syrup by cooking 2 cups sugar with 1 ½ cups water. Add ginger slices to flavor. Cook over medium heat for about 10 minutes until thickened to a maple syrup consistency. Discard ginger slices.

2. Heat enough oil in large pan to fry rice cakes. Typically, these are twice-fried: first at a lower temperature to cook through and then at a higher temperature to brown and crisp. If frying twice, start in 275-degree oil, cooking cakes in batches of about 10 minutes each. Drain and cool slightly, then heat oil to 325 degrees and cook cakes again for a minute or two, turning to brown all sides. Transfer to paper towels or brown paper bag to drain.
3. Coat fried rice cakes in sugar syrup, then roll in sesame seeds.

Yumil-gwa (Fried Dough Sweet)

This is similar to the previous recipe, but with wheat dough and honey syrup.

- Prep & Cooking Time: 45 minutes
- For 10 servings

Nutrition Info per serving

- Calories 460
- Fat 13g
- Carbohydrates 85g
- Sodium 4mg

Ingredients

- 2 cups plus 1/3 cup honey, divided
- 3 thick slices ginger
- 3 cups all-purpose flour
- 1/3 cup rice wine
- 1/3 cup toasted sesame oil

- ¼ cup finely ground pine nuts plus additional whole for garnish
- Neutral oil, for frying

Preparation

1. Put 2 cups honey and 2 cups water in small saucepan to make syrup. Add ginger slices. Cook at medium for 10 minutes, until thickened. Discard ginger slices.
2. Make the dough by mixing all remaining ingredients, including additional 1/3 cup honey, excepting whole nuts and oil. Roll dough into a rough square about 1/3 inch thick, cut into 2-3 inch cookies, using a cookie cutter or small glass.
3. Typically, these are twice-fried: first at a lower temperature to cook through and then at a higher temperature to brown and crisp. If frying twice, start in 275-degree oil, cooking cakes in batches for about 2-3 minutes a side. Drain and cool slightly, then heat oil to 325 degrees and cook cakes again for a minute or two, turning to brown all sides. Transfer to paper towels or brown paper bag to drain.
4. Toss cookies with honey syrup then sprinkle whole pine nuts over. You can also press whole nuts into the surface of the cookie while warm, making a design.

Kkultarae (King's Candy)

This is a deceptively simple recipe with tasty and fun results if you persevere. The end result should be somewhat like thicker, chewier cotton candy.

- Prep & Cook Time: 2 hours (includes cooling time)
- Yield: About a pound

Nutrition Info per serving

- Calories 295
- Fat 0 g
- Carbohydrates 77 g
- Sodium 1 mg

Ingredients

- 2 cups cornstarch
- 2 ½ cups sugar
- ¼ cup of corn syrup
- 2 tbsp of rice wine vinegar
- Food coloring, if you like

Preparation

1. Cook cornstarch over medium heat in a large pan for 10 minutes. Spread out on a baking sheet and reserve.
2. Bring corn syrup and sugar, vinegar, and ¾ cup water to a boil in a pot. Boil until mixture attains 250 degrees on a thermometer (a candy thermometer is best).

3. Pour into doughnut-shaped molds, preferably silicone, and chill in the refrigerator for an hour.
4. xxPop candy out of molds, and roll in reserved cornstarch. Then, pull into string-like candy: with your hands, spread into a wide ring, twist to make a new ring, then pull again. Continue pulling and twisting to make longer and thinner threads of candy. Repeat.

Yeot-gangjeong (Sesame Candy)

- Prep & Cooking Time: 15 minutes
- For 4 servings

Nutrition Info per serving

- Calories 383
- Fat 26 g
- Carbohydrates 33.6 g
- Sodium 7 mg

Ingredients

- 3 tbsp honey
- 3 tbsp sugar
- 1 cup sesame seeds, toasted
- ¼ cup roasted, unsalted nuts (peanuts are traditional, but any nut you like will work)

Preparation

1. Bring honey, sugar, 1 tbsp water, and a touch of salt to boil. Boil for about 3 minutes, then stir in seeds and nuts.
2. Turn out onto parchment paper and shape with an oiled rolling pin into a ½ inch thick rectangle or square. Let cool slightly, then cut into shapes or squares with a sharp knife (dip knife in cold water between slicing to keep the mixture from sticking).

Tteok

Tteok is a category of sweets made of various kinds of rice cakes. They can be steamed, pounded, shaped, or pan-fried. See below for some recipes and methods for making tteok at home.

Steamed Tteok

Kongtteok (Bean tteok)

- Cook & Prep Time: 45 min. plus soak time
- Yield: 10 servings

Nutrition Info per serving

- Calories 372
- Fat 11 g
- Carbohydrates 55 g
- Sodium 21 mg

Ingredients

- 1 cup black soybeans
- 5 cups sweet rice flour
- 2 tbsp sugar
- ½ cup dried raisins or cranberries
- 1 cup walnuts

Preparation

1. Soak dried beans for 4 hours.

2. Mix defrosted sweet rice flour with sugar, breaking up any clumps. Stir in remaining ingredients, and place mixture in a steamer lined with cheesecloth. Steam for 30 minutes.
3. Wait until cool, then invert the rice cake onto a cutting board so you can slice into wedges.

Jeungpyeon (Rice wine tteok)

These are special occasion rice cakes for the harvest moon festival in Korea. Filled and shaped, often elaborately decorated, they are complicated to make. Below is a more accessible version for this tasty treat.

- Cook & Prep Time: 1 hr.
- Yield: 15 filled cakes

Nutrition Info per serving

- Calories 582
- Fat 13.4 g
- Carbohydrates 55 g
- Sodium 1 mg

Ingredients

- 3 cups sweet rice flour
- 3 tbsp honey
- 4 tbsp pine nuts, coarsely crushed
- 4 tbsp sesame seeds, toasted and coarsely crushed
- Pine needles, optional
- 1 tbsp toasted sesame oil

Preparation

1. Mix flour with ½ cup water and knead until smooth, around 2 minutes.
2. To make the filling, mix pine nuts with half of the honey in one small bowl; mix sesame seeds with half of the honey

in another small bowl. Take 1 ounce of dough, roll into a ball, then make a well in the center and put in a tsp or two of filling. Shape ball around filling.

3. When all dough and filling have been used, place dough balls in a steamer lined with cheesecloth (and covered with pine needles, if using) and steam for 0 minutes. When done, remove to a serving tray and brush with sesame oil.

Baekseolgi (Raisin tteok)

- Cook & Prep Time: 40 min.
- Yield: 8 servings

Nutrition Info per serving

- Calories 506
- Fat 8 g
- Carbohydrates 85 g
- Sodium 2 mg

Ingredients

- 4 cups sweet rice flour
- ¼ cup of sugar
- 1-2 cups of dried fruits and sliced or chopped nuts (raisins, apricots, cranberries, almonds, pine nuts, walnuts)

Preparation

1. Put defrosted rice flour in a bowl and break up any lumps. Be sure it is fluffy then add sugar. Sift ingredients together.
2. Line a steamer basket with cheesecloth and place an 8-inch cake ring into the basket. Pack rice flour mixture into cake ring, then top with dried fruits and nuts.
3. Steam for 30 minutes then cool for a bit before lifting out of the steamer and removing cake ring. Serve immediately.

Pounded Tteok

Injeolmi (Sweet Beantteok)

- Cook & Prep Time: 15 min.
- Yield: 8-10 cakes

Nutrition Info per serving

- Calories 371
- Fat 2 g
- Carbohydrates 82 g
- Sodium 50 mg

Ingredients

- 1 cup sweet rice flour
- 1 tbsp sugar
- Pinch of salt
- ¾ cup of water
- ½ cup roasted soybean powder

Preparation

1. Mix rice flour, sugar, salt, and water in a microwave-safe bowl. Be sure to cover tightly with plastic wrap and microwave on for 3 minutes at high power. Stir ingredients again, then microwave again for 1 minute.
2. Put the hot dough into a mortar or other sturdy bowl and pound at least 50 times, about a minute or two, until the texture is chewy.
3. Form into 8-10 cakes, roll in roasted soybean powder. Add another sprinkle of sugar before serving, if you like.

Kkaeinjeolmi (Black Sesame tteok)

Follow recipe for Injeolmi above, substituting black sesame seeds for roasted soybean powder.

Danpatjuk (Sweet Bean & Rice Dumpling Soup)

- Prep & Cook Time: 1 ½ hr.
- Yield: 8 servings

Nutrition Info per serving

- Calories 347
- Fat 0 g
- Carbohydrates 78 g
- Sodium 319 mg

Ingredients

- 1 cup red beans
- 1-2 cups brown sugar, divided
- 1 tsp cinnamon
- 1 tsp salt
- 1 cup sweet rice flour
- Pine nuts, for garnish

Preparation

1. Cook red beans in water to cover until tender, about 1 hour. Drain and mash beans to a paste (or pulse them in

a food processor). Mix bean paste with 1 cup of brown sugar, salt, and cinnamon. Set aside.
2. Make rice balls by mixing sweet rice flour with 1 tbsp sugar and add ½ cup of water to form a dough (add up to ½ cup more water if the mixture is dry). Form into ½ inch balls.
3. Put bean paste, 4 cups water, another ½ cup or more sugar and bring to a boil. Ladle in rice balls and cook until done around 10 minutes. Ladle into bowls and garnish with pine nuts.

Shaped Tteok

Songpyeon (Half-moon stuffed tteok)

- Prep & Cook Time: 2 hours
- Yield: 30 filled cakes

Nutrition Info per serving

- Calories 259
- Fat 3.2 g
- Carbohydrates 52.3 g
- Sodium 1 mg

Ingredients

- 2 pounds frozen rice flour, divided (optional)
- Water

For Filling:

- ½ cup sesame seeds
- 2 tbsp sugar
- 1 tbsp honey

Preparation

1. Most cooks will color their dough with natural dyes that also add a touch of flavor, such as blueberry juice, raspberry juice, or green tea powder. This can also be achieved with a few drops of food coloring, or it can be skipped altogether.

2. To make the dough, mix 2 cups rice flour with 4 tbsp liquid (water or juice), adding more liquid to form a shapeable dough. If making various colors, you should have enough to make 3 different colors in addition to plain. Let dough rest for 30 minutes.
3. Meanwhile, make filling: toast sesame seeds in a pan for roughly 5 minutes, taking care not to burn. Grind seeds finely, either in spice/coffee grinder or with mortar &pestle. Mix with sugar and honey.
4. Pinch off enough dough to make a 1-inch ball, make a well in the center, then add ½ tsp of filling, then shape dough around filling to make a half moon shape. Repeat with remaining dough and filling.
5. Line steamer basket with cheesecloth and steam filled cakes for 20 minutes. Don't allow cakes to touch each other; steam in batches if necessary.

Baram Tteok (Round stuffed tteok)

- Prep & Cook Time: 30 min.
- Yield: 16 balls

Ingredients

- 2 cups glutinous rice flour
- 7 tbsp sugar
- 1 tsp salt
- Food coloring, optional
- 1 ½ cup adzuki (red bean) paste: can be purchased at Asian markets or made at home; see danpatjuk recipe for directions)
- Cornstarch

Preparation

1. Mix rice flour, sugar, and salt with 1 cup water in microwave safe bowl (you can add food coloring here if you like). Microwave for 3 minutes on high power. Remove and stir for another 3 minutes, creating an elastic dough.
2. Divide red bean paste into 16 ping pong sized balls and set aside.
3. Divide dough into two equal portions and shape into long cylinders, then divide into 8 equal pieces each. Wrap dough around red bean balls and seal. Roll each in cornstarch.

Pan Fried Tteok

Hwajeon (Flower tteok)

- Prep & Cook Time: 30 min.
- Yield: 6 cakes

Ingredients

- Calories 169
- Fat 3.5 g
- Carbohydrates 33 g
- Sodium 0 mg

Ingredients

- 3 tbsp sugar
- ½ cup sweet rice flour
- 2 tsps neutral oil
- Edible flowers

Preparation

1. Mix 3 tbsp sugar with 3 tbsp water and cook over medium heat in a small saucepan until a syrup is formed about 5 minutes.
2. Mix sweet rice flour with a dash of salt and ¼ cup nearly boiling water. Knead the dough until it is smooth, then divide into 6 portions of equal size. Press each piece into a 2 inch round cake.

3. Heat oil in large pan (you don't want cakes touching). Fry cakes over low heat, in order to keep their white color, for about 4-5 minutes per side. When cooked through and slightly crispy, press an edible flower on top of the cake and flip gently, cooking for a few seconds to help the flour adhere to the cake. Serve immediately.

Bukkumi (Filled Crescent tteok)

- Prep & Cook Time: 40 min.
- Yield: 4 servings

Ingredients

- 1 cup sweet rice flour
- 1/3 cup hot water
- 8 ounces red bean paste (available in some markets, or made from scratch as in danpatjuk recipe)
- 2 tbsp neutral oil
- 1 tbsp toasted sesame oil
- Pumpkin seeds, for garnish (optional)

Preparation

1. Mix 1 cup rice flour with water to make dough. If additional water needed, add. Knead for about 5 minutes, set aside to rest for 5-10 minutes.
2. Divide dough into 4 pieces of equal weight and roll each piece into a 5 inch round. Put 2 tbsp of red bean paste in the center, and fold dough over to create a crescent shape. Seal well.
3. Heat both oils in a large skillet and fry crescents 1-2 minutes a side. Press 2 or 3 pumpkin seeds in each crescent for garnish, if you like.

Drinks

Cha (Tea)

Tea is adored across the world, but perhaps no more so than in Asia. Korea has its own tea traditions and history, and Koreans happily make tea from any number of ingredients. See below for how to make three of the mostpopular types of tea drinks.

Green Tea: How to Brew

Method

Many people tend to brew the delicate green tea at higher temperatures than is advisable. For best results, steep 1 heaping tsp of loose green tea leaves in 1 cup of water warmed to 145 degrees. Steep for 4-5 minutes. Often, higher quality tea is steeped in minimally warmed water 2 or 3 times in order to bloom the delicate, complex flavor.

Barley Tea: How to Brew

Method

Koreans drink barley tea as a digestive aid, as well as for its uniquely nutty taste. Toast ¼ whole (not pearled) barley in a medium hot skillet for about 10 minutes. Meanwhile, bring about 1 quart of water to a boil. When barley is done toasting, add it to the water and lower heat. Bring to a bare simmer for 15 minutes, then strain. This tea is lovely served with a touch of honey to sweeten. This technique is also used with brown rice.

Fruit Teas: How to Brew

There are numerous fruit infusions, loosely categorized as teas, enjoyed throughout Korea and Asia in general. Brewing a fruit tea from fresh fruit is almost always superior to using "flavored" teas that you may find in the grocery store. Some of the most common in Korea are jujube tea, plum tea, and ginseng tea. These "teas" are not made with green or black tea, but as their names suggest are the brewed essences of the main ingredient. One very popular tea, Yuja cha (Citron tea) is often consumed to promote good health. See below for method.

Method
Scrub the peels of 5 citrons (yuzu) fruits and cut into thin slices, then quarter slices. Remove seeds but leave peel. Dissolve ¾ cup honey in a ¼ cup of nearly boiling water and stir. Add citron and crush fruit slightly to release flavors. Leave it to sit for a day, then refrigerate and use for tea: 1-2 tbsp citron marmalade per 1 cup hot water. If you cannot find fresh citrons, you can often find already prepared citron marmalade in Korean markets.

Cinnamon Tea

Method

Combine 8 sticks of cinnamon with 1 quart of water and ½ cup sugar. Heat to a boil, then lower heat and simmer for about 20 minutes. Fish out the cinnamon sticks and serve. This tea is often served cold, garnished with a spoonful of pine nuts.

Non-Alcoholic Drinks

Sujeonggwa (Cinnamon Ginger Punch)

Method:

Simmer about 20 cinnamon sticks in 11 cups of water for 40 minutes. In a separate pot, simmer 2 or 3 large pieces of ginger, peeled, in 11 cups of water for 40 minutes. Put 2 ½ cups sugar in another large pot, then strain cinnamon and ginger water into that and simmer until sugar is dissolved and flavors meld, about 20 minutes more. This is usually served cold, even slushy, garnished with dried fruits and nuts. Makes 20 servings.

Subak Hwachae (Watermelon Punch)

Method:

Ball or cube 4 cups watermelon (use a variety, if you like, of red and yellow watermelon or some honeydew for a visually stunning presentation). Using scraps from watermelons, puree enough to make about ½ cup juice, sieved if you like, and add to balls. Pour over 2 cups ginger ale, 2 cups strawberry milk, OR a mix of both to equal 2 cups. Stir in 3 tbsp mild vinegar or lime juice. Serve with ice cubes and a spoon to slurp up the watermelon. Garnish with other fresh fruit, such as pineapple and blueberry, if you like, and some fresh mint. Makes 4-5 servings.

Sikhye (Sweet Rice Drink)

Method:

Make barley tea, either following the above method or by using malted barley tea bags, often found in Asian grocery stores. You need about 8 ounces of tea bags to 15 cups of water (or, alternately, 15 cups of homemade barley tea). Place barley tea (or bags in water) in an oven safe dish; add 1 cup cooked short grain rice. Put in oven at its lowest setting for about 4 hours. Strain out bags, if using, and rice. Set rice aside. Heat steeped liquid with 1 cup of sugar until sugar is dissolved, then cool in refrigerator. Serve with a scoop of reserved rice and some toasted pine nuts. Makes 12 servings or more.

Alcoholic Drinks

Sul is the general name for alcoholic spirits in Korea. There are many categories, including rice wine (clear, milky, or flavored), distilled liquors such as soju, and beer. There is a traditional etiquette surrounding drinking in Korean culture, as well: be sure to pour for your elders and to receive a drink with both hands. Below are some traditional and not so traditional recipes for using Korean style spirits in your evening aperitif.

Soju Yogurt Cocktail

Method:

Soju, a grain spirit similar to vodka, lends itself well to a variety of cocktails. One popular in Korea is made with yogurt: for one drink, in a cocktail shaker, shake soju with 3 ounces prepared yogurt drink (such as lassi or kefir) and 3 ounces lemon-lime soda. To change it up, use a flavored yogurt drink and garnish with fresh fruit.

Soju is also sometimes mixed with cola, fruit juices, or tonic.

Flavored Liquors

Method:

Flavoring liquors or fermenting fruit from the vine is found the world around. Flavored liquors or wines can be found pre-made in establishments selling Korean spirits, but it can also be done at home. Pour a standard sized bottle of soju (750 milliliters) into a large container with a lid. Add ¼ sugar and about 1 cup of whatever fresh fruit you have on hand; let steep for at least two weeks, then strain. Popular fruits include citron (yuzu), raspberries, apples, and pears. Use what looks best! This method can also be used with rice wine, though reduce sugar to 2 tbsp.

Ginger Cocktail

Method:

While not traditional to Korean culture, both ginger and soju are prevalent in Korean cuisine. Ginger is thought to aid digestion, so this cocktail would make an excellent digestive. Make sugar syrup using ½ cup sugar, ½ cup water, and 3 or 4 slices of ginger: bring to a bare simmer in a saucepan for about 5 minutes, then cool and discard ginger slices. For one drink, mix 2-3 tbsps of ginger syrup, ½ cup soju, and squeeze of lemon or lime juice. Serve over ice, topped with a bit of sparkling soda water, if you like.

Conclusion

I hope you have enjoyed the vicarious experience of traveling through Korea. Often times, it is through food and a culinary tradition that one can get the best sense of a people and their culture. As the famous chef, Jean-Anthelme Brillat-Savarin reportedly noted, "Tell me what you eat, and I'll tell you who you are." We are lucky to live in a time in which we have access to a global pantry and a wide knowledge of various cuisines throughout the world. Korean food is a unique and hearty contribution to the world stage, a relative newcomer to the American market but a quickly growing standard.

Korean food is also healthy and vibrant, a break from the usual American meal, with its predominantly spicy and fermented flavors. With its emphasis on balance and in utilizing all five tastes, this kind of cooking is as intriguing as it is healthy—and, most recipes are quite simple to make at home, even without access to a specialty market.

The Korean meal is meant to be shared, family style, and brings people around the table to enjoy a meal together—a fading tradition that deserves a revival. With a pot of stew or a plate of grilled meat, some rice, kimchi, and a handful of banchan, you can explore a whole new world with your loved ones. Don't forget the tea and cakes!